T0003100

MORNING *and*
EVENING PRAYERS

MORNING *and* EVENING PRAYERS

Cornelius Plantinga

WILLIAM B. EERDMANS PUBLISHING COMPANY
GRAND RAPIDS, MICHIGAN

Wm. B. Eerdmans Publishing Co.
4035 Park East Court SE, Grand Rapids, Michigan 49546
www.eerdmans.com

27 26 25 24 23 22 21   1 2 3 4 5 6 7

ISBN 978-0-8028-7881-6

Library of Congress Cataloging-in-Publication Data

Names: Plantinga, Cornelius, 1946– author.
Title: Morning and evening prayers / Cornelius Plantinga.
Description: Grand Rapids, Michigan : William B.
    Eerdmans Publishing Company, [2021] | Summary:
    "A compilation of prayers centered on basic Christian
    longings, intended to be used daily in the morning and
    evening"—Provided by publisher.
Identifiers: LCCN 2020051108 | ISBN 9780802878816
Subjects: LCSH: Prayers.
Classification: LCC BV245 .P53 2021 |
    DDC 242/.2—dc23
LC record available at https://lccn.loc.gov/2020051108

For Kathleen

Introduction

A lot of us pray on our own. We pour out our thoughts and feelings to a listening God. We praise and thank God. We confess to God. We ask God for things. And it's entirely natural to do so. How else would we maintain fellowship with God?

But, some of the time, others pray on our behalf. A spouse, a family member, a friend, or our pastor prays, and we listen and endorse in our minds and hearts. We pray vicariously. Some of the prayers on our behalf get published. Think of the Book of Common Prayer, with its glorious addresses to God. Think of John Baillie's *Diary of Private Prayer*, with its one month's worth of morning and evening prayers. Think of many of the psalms, of Paul's prayers, of the Lord's Prayer.

In a lifetime of devotions, I have used others' prayers quite a bit. I pray words of a psalm or hymn or spiritual song. I pray John Baillie's prayers for a month and then, six months later, pray them again. I pray the Lord's Prayer virtually every day. Sometimes I pray silently and sometimes aloud. Often, I choose a wonderful sentence from someone else's prayer, memorize it, and thread it through my day. If, say, a John Baillie prayer is laid out in paragraphs, I may choose to pray just one or two of the paragraphs and save the others for subsequent days.

You will have your own reasons for using published prayers. Here are four of mine.

First, other people's prayers jog me out of my rut. I use them to ask for things I hadn't thought to ask for. I thank God for things I had entirely overlooked. I intercede for some kinds of people I had lamentably ignored. On the spot, my prayer life expands.

Second, my spiritual life sometimes flags. Doubts nag at me. Energy fails me. Spiritual depression drags on me. But these same things happened to some of the psalmists. If I pray one of their prayers, I feel bonded and understood. I feel as if I'm in a fellowship of flaggers and that God still wants to hear from all of us.

Third, some of us go through trauma that silences our prayers. Wary and numb, we go mute. How wonderful, then, that others keep right on praying for us and that we can silently join them.

Finally, certain forms of prayer cry out for company. They're not meant to be prayed alone. That's why psalmists keep calling to others to praise God *with* them. They call not only to themselves ("Praise the Lord, O my soul"), but also to angels, shining stars, fire and hail, mountains and cattle, old people and young people together. "Let them praise the name of the LORD, for . . . his glory is above earth and heaven."*
If I use a published prayer to join this great chorus of witnesses, I will be powerfully uplifted. And if I use a published prayer to lead others in prayer, they may be uplifted too.

* Psalm 148:13 NRSV.

What follows is a month of morning and evening prayers, with a concluding prayer suitable for use on a Sunday. You will notice that some prayers use the first-person-singular pronoun. It is I who pray. But some use the first-person-plural pronoun. It is we who pray. I want first-person-singular praying because it allows for more intimacy. I want first-person-plural prayers because they let me pray from the company of all believers. It is I who pray, yes, but not as a stand-alone Christian. I pray only as a member of the church and her fellowship.

The pages include a number of empty spaces. You may want to use them for notes, or to add a pertinent verse of Scripture, or to lay down your own additional praise, petition, or thanksgiving. Or you may want to urge yourself on. As in so many spiritual things, the ability to pray, especially in times of trouble, is God's gift. But the resolve to pray is our calling.

In the collection that follows, if any prayer seems too long, break it up and try it in shorter lengths. On some days it's just what's needed. In any case, I hope that just as others' prayers have helped me, some of the ones that follow may help you.

MORNING *and*
EVENING PRAYERS

Morning

Faithful God, I have awakened to your new day. Let me rejoice and be glad in it. I turn to you at its threshold because I depend completely on your strength. I have not made myself, cannot keep myself, could never save myself. And so, loving God, I give myself to you for this day—my creator, keeper, and savior.

Thank you that I may awaken refreshed from a night's sleep, that I may awaken alert and ready for what the day may bring. Thank you that I may today hear your name on the lips of people I love. Thank you for all your gifts that come clearly marked as gifts—

> nourishing food and nourishing friends
> work to do and energy to do it
> wonderful expressions
>   on the faces of children
> your love that speaks my name and looks for me
>   with eyes that have longing in them

Surely your goodness is beyond all thinking and beyond all telling.

But thank you this morning also for gifts that arrive under wraps. Today I may be interrupted and annoyed, only to discover later that the interruption was entirely necessary for my growth. I may be vexed by a difficult person I later find to have been my teacher. I may feel your absence and find myself pining for you even more.

O God, in your mercy tend to the church across the world today. Tend to all of us pastors and members, worship leaders and musicians, council members and custodians. I confess to you that we often preach a better gospel than we live. I confess to you how often we are tempted to use the gospel for entertainment, or for making money, or for molding others to our will. Forgive us. Then revive us and make us strong, so that we may serve your purposes and add luster to your reputation and bring joy into all the precincts of heaven.

I start this day, good God, confessing that I did not make myself, cannot keep myself, could never save myself. And so, I turn to you—my maker, keeper, and savior through Jesus Christ. *Amen.*

Evening

There's a wideness in your mercy, O God, and a kindness in your justice. Wider and deeper than the oceans, your mercy stretches from everlasting to everlasting. Firm to the end, your justice persists just because you love so deeply. There is none like you.

Saving God, from you comes every kindness that surprises and lifts. You are the one willing to suffer so I may be healed, willing to stoop so I may stand straight. You have served me even when I was unwilling to serve you. Right through my ups and downs your love has always endured.

How I have needed it today! Eternal God, always alert, you have searched me and known me. You know my pious boredom and quiet spiritual neglect. You know how keenly I hunger not for righteousness, but for success. You know how often my fine words hide a shabby heart.

I seek your face, now, on behalf of your children across the world. Search and destroy in us all that chokes the breath of your Spirit. Search and destroy all that starves the Pentecostal flame. Flare in us again, bringing purity, peace, and the glorious freedom of the children of God.

Now, for good friends to cheer us, for seasonal weather to envelop us, for good work to engage us, we give you thanks. For families who love us and work-people who help us and wise colleagues who advise us—for hope not just of pleasure but also of joy—I join all your children to give you hearty thanks. You have often kept us safe from accidents and from deadly diseases even when we weren't thinking of you. You have preserved us from the deadly slide into unbelief even when we weren't aware of the anchors that secure us.

Before I lie down to sleep, I commend all your children to your tender care. Be present with those who watch, or wake, or weep tonight, and give your angels charge over those who sleep.

> Tend your sick ones, good God.
> Rest your weary ones.
> Bless your dying ones.
> Soothe your suffering ones.
> Shield your joyous ones—
>   all for your own love's sake.* *Amen.*

* Saint Augustine's prayer paraphrased from *Book of Common Worship, Daily Prayer* (Louisville: Westminster John Knox, 1993), 119.

Morning

Lord Jesus Christ, from whom angels hide their faces, you came to be with us sinners. You are King of kings, and yet you humbled yourself to bear our flesh. You shine with heavenly glory, and yet you lowered yourself into our darkness. You radiate moral purity, and yet you absorbed all our evil into your holy being and did not pass evil back.

We, your followers, live in a world that frightens us in so many ways. Wind and lashing storms menace us. Rising oceans and greenhouse gases alarm us. A whole world of bacteria and viruses threatens us. Some of us are sick. Some of us have been sick. Some of us will be sick. All of us are afraid of being sick. Save us.

You entered our world as a helpless babe. This morning I lift to you the babies of the world who cannot do for themselves, and the elderly, who can now do so much less for themselves than before. I lift to you the impoverished, the unlettered, the unheard, the unmentioned, the unemployed, the unemployable.

You were a homeless man with no place to lay your head. Please look in favor on the exiled peoples of the world. Look in mercy on men and women in refugee camps today, dependent for life itself on blessed hand-outs. Look in mercy on their children, stung to see their parents beg strangers for help. Turn the strangers into

6

friends, and the camps into havens of relief, all because your own people knew exile and because you are the one in whom our hearts find their true home. But don't let us pass off to you the problems we ourselves could join you in addressing. Meanwhile,

> shine everlasting light on us,
> rain unceasing bounty on us,
> blow life-giving love on us, and
> settle refreshing dew on us.

Shine on us, rain on us, blow on us, settle on us. Lord Jesus Christ, Savior of the world, your followers need you. Come into our lives today. Hosanna. Save us. *Amen.*

Evening

Lord God, you transcend the furthest reach of human thinking, and yet you dwell in human hearts. You are deeply hidden and yet most intimately present. You govern the great movements of human history, and yet, this very day, you have also governed my little acts.

Now let your light shine into every dingy corner of my life. Clear away the webs of doubt and the wisps of unbelief. Establish me, O God, firm as rock along the streets and ways of your kingdom. Be present with me through the watches of this night and go with me through the bustle of each day. Merciful God, I have no adequacy of my own and no resources for the task unless you give them.

All your people pray to you tonight. We bring you thanks for human love that can be old and deep, for people who may be trusted with our secrets, for children who are delightful in ways we could never fully describe. We give you thanks, O God,

> for strong and caring teachers
> for church staff members
>   and their faithful ministry
> for those among us who sing and play music

for all whose work is a magnet that pulls us
toward your splendor

Especially, we thank you for Jesus Christ and for his terrible death and startling resurrection.

Before I lay my head on my pillow, I commend to your care all who have today worked in Christ's name.

Shelter them.
Support them.
Befriend them.
Erect your arch of blessing over them.

I commend to you those across the world who learn languages and build churches and struggle for justice. Touch them with your favor. To all who faithfully nurse loved ones, or who lead the way through the labyrinths of government bureaucracy, or who speak in the name of Christ against human evil, give strength and the quiet confidence that even when no one else notices, and no one else applauds, still all heaven rejoices because once more, across the world, your kingdom comes and your will is done in Jesus's name. *Amen.*

Morning

Your name, O God, is your alter ego.

Your name is your reputation.
Your name is a magnet for prayer.
Your name has your glory in it.

Let me live today to praise your holy name. Let my actions witness to eternity.

Please let me be more patient today. Let me live gladly in the present. The future beckons me, draws me, summons me. Let me resist its pull. Let me dwell restfully in the present, waiting calmly for the future to arrive.

Make me patient today. Let me absorb nuisances without fussing over them:

> poky drivers in the left lane
> people who let their dog bark all night
> rude salesclerks and rude customers

Let me be patient with irritating strangers. But also with my loved ones. Let me be OK with

> their annoying facial expressions
>   and tones of voice
> their hastiness or lethargy

the way they jump to conclusions
the way they simply can't decide anything

O God, I need to be more patient. I need to absorb irritants without getting paralyzed by them. Patience is fruit of the Spirit, and I'm asking for it now. There's so much anger in the world. Angry politics, angry talk shows, angry online back-and-forth, music with an attitude. So much anger, and I don't want to add anything to it. I want patience, good God, because it's a virtue that fits those who have been raised with Christ. It's part of the family uniform of your people.

Give me a long fuse and a short memory where irritants are concerned. Make me hard to provoke. Not stoic, not naïve, just hard to provoke. I may still get good and angry at injustice. After all, I'd be imitating you. I'm asking for patience, not complacence. Patience to rebuke calmly. Patience to forgive gracefully. Patience in case I can get no justice at all.

O God, make me more patient today for Jesus's sake. *Amen.*

Evening

O God, so many of us are full of fear. But we are also full of your love. We are afraid of growing old and weak. But your love is enough. We are afraid of sinning our way right to the edge of desperation. But your love is enough. We are afraid of the dark, afraid of sleepless nights, afraid of a runaway virus, afraid of being afraid. But your love is enough.

The night is upon me, and I have not yet fulfilled your hopes for me today. I have fallen short once again.

> I have not loved you with everything I have.
> I have not loved my neighbor as myself.
> I have not examined myself
>   or properly confessed my sins.
> I have been too slow, too hesitant,
>   too short on bravery.

I am in so many ways an unprofitable servant. But I am *your* servant. So, before I sleep, I surrender myself once again to your love, which I know is enough.

Revealing God, you speak in the daily circuit of the earth and in the regular sequence of light and darkness. You speak in the stars that shine and in the moon that glows with ghostly light. You speak through your law, as regular in its ways as sun, moon, and earth. Thank you for the stars and moon that speak your greatness, and for your law that speaks your wisdom.*

Original fountain of goodness, I have no goodness of my own. Any authentic word I speak I first heard from you. Any leading of the lost is by your map. Any food I offer comes from shelves you stocked. Fill me with your fullness, Lord, until my heart overflows, until my heart naturally overflows.

Meanwhile, loose me from easy answers and false securities. Remind me that only your strong arm can save. Inspire me to encourage the listless and to bind up the brokenhearted.

Tonight, wonderful God,

> let your love be my pillow,
> let your Spirit be my comforter, and
> let your forgiveness be my bed of rest,
>   through Jesus Christ. *Amen.*

* This paragraph is based loosely on Psalm 19.

Morning

fourth day

Holy God, you who love the good and speak the truth, look in mercy on us sinners.

> We love the good and speak the truth
>   when it's convenient.
> We love the good and speak the truth
>   when it's profitable.
> We love the good and speak the truth
>   when it's noticeable.

O God, holy beyond our thought, we do not belong in your fellowship except that, in your goodness, it is a fellowship provided explicitly for sinners, a fellowship of mercy.

Honest God, I want purity of heart. I want integrity. As I move through this day, I want to ring true wherever you tap me. I don't want to try to remember my lies, and which lies I told to which people. I don't want to lie at all. I don't want to pretend to be sincere. I want to be sincere. I don't want to contradict myself and then try to explain to somebody what I was really saying. I want to say things straight in the first place.

Good God, give me purity of heart today. Let my yes be yes and let my no be no.* Let my heart be all of

* Matthew 5:37.

14

one piece. Let me be just this, not this-and-that. Please keep me from a divided life, a two-faced life, a double life. Let me be all me, the new me, the only me that has been raised with Jesus.

Holy God, I keep trying to compartmentalize my life. I store my honesty in one spot and my dishonesty in another, my compassion in one place and my indifference in another.

Correct me. Unite me. Pull me apart and put me back together the right way. Let me be whole. And give me an honest willingness to examine myself in the light of your Word.

I don't need to be always serene, gracious God. I can live with the drag of doubt. I can push on through spiritual depression. But only if you go with me through the doubt and depression, only if you are at my side and in my heart.

Honest God, let me be honest today for Jesus's sake. *Amen.*

Evening

Wonderful God, I have not achieved my faith but discovered it. You have approached me in a hundred ways, and I have found myself trusting you.

> You have made me for your company
> and pleasure.
> You have made me for praying
> and singing to you.
> You have sent me out as your witness
> in the world.

I have tried to make you predictable. But you are the God of thunder. I have tried to make you domestic. But you are the God of galaxies. I have tried to tame you. But you are the God who makes mountains tremble.

Let me know the greatness of your power, but also the greatness of your love.

I join my voice with so many others to bring you thanks. Life under your canopy can be rich with music and laughter, food and friends, sunsets and seascapes, fulfilling worship with people we love. Thank you. Every song of a lark, every scent of a flower, every touch of a child suggests your goodness. Every word of forgiveness or assurance expresses your grace.

But I also join my voice with so many others to lament our misery. Life under your canopy can be deeply distressing—so disordered, so empty of leadership, goals, purposes. Chaos is miserable, O God. Life can be so lonely for those who lack warm friends and faithful family members. Loneliness is miserable, O God. Life can be so full of want for people who lack safe housing, stable income, dependable health insurance. Poverty is miserable, O God. People are crying out. Please come to help. Saving is your specialty. Please do it. And enlist us in the project. In your presence, we should not just agonize. We should organize.

Lord Jesus Christ, Son of God, your feet took you to lepers, and your hands touched flesh otherwise untouchable. Your knees bent so you could wash the feet of disciples who hadn't dreamed of doing it for each other. Your arms stretched wide enough on the cross to embrace the world. Son of God, saving is your specialty. Please do it. And enlist us in the project. *Amen.*

Morning

G enerous God, overflowing fountain of good, you have lived from all eternity in triune abundance. For your fulfillment you did not need to make anything, and yet you have made room in the universe for creatures, creating life through the mediating Son and the hovering Spirit, pouring out value on all that you made.

You honored us human beings with the breath of your life, making us in your image and likeness to care for the earth in stewardship and love, to live together in hospitality and zest as a small duplicate of your interpersonal fullness.

You crowned us with virtue and are now renewing us in your image through the work of your Son. Magnificent you are, strong God, giver of splendors we could no more have conceived than deserved.

> You bless inside a world of curses.
> You heal inside a world of wounds.
> You save inside a world of loss.

We thank, praise, and honor you, generous God, overflowing fountain of good, through Jesus Christ, our Lord. You dwell beyond all worlds and stars and yet are secretly present to human hearts. You shine with purity and glory, lighting up ranks of angels and archangels, and yet you dwell in the dark places with sinners like me.

Now I pause at the threshold of this new day to acclaim your great salvation. You rescue your people from sin and death through the mighty work of Jesus your Son. You pour out your Spirit on the church. You send evangelists to the world with the gospel. You raise up prophets to cry for justice. You give martyrs their comfort and saints their heavenly rest. You are a God of unending mercy.

Lord Jesus Christ, Son of God, I'm thinking today of family and friends, and of believers across the world.

> Let whatever is ugly in us become small.
> Let whatever is beautiful become large.
> Let our fears become small.
> Let our confidence in you become large.

Shrink our pride; enlarge our humility; shrink our envy; enlarge our gratitude. Rise above our pettiness, O Lord Christ. Rise above our sorrows and fears and let us rise with you. *Amen.*

Evening

G reat God, master of the universe:

> choirs of angels sing for you,
> saints and martyrs adore you,
> trees clap their hands to applaud you, and
> mountains skip like rams, and little hills like
> lambs, to celebrate you.*

All earth and heaven rejoice at your majesty. Glory, hallelujah!

I pause now to ask you to sift my thoughts, weigh my words, sort my deeds of today. Bury whatever was unworthy. Lift to highest heaven whatever was worthy. I am a sinner, greatly in need of your saving grace, but that's not all I am. I am also your beloved child to whom you have promised saving grace. I claim your promise, God, and take it to my heart.

Spirit of all comfort, you know us human beings. You know our fears and our sadness. You hear the cries of anguish around the world. Look tonight with compassion on those who suffer hunger, including so many precious children. Look in mercy on work slaves and

* Echoes here of Psalm 114:4 and Isaiah 55:14.

sex slaves and on all victims of persecution. Embrace the world's persecuted Christians, who suffer just for bearing the name of Christ. Heal the sick, good God, including those sick of soul or sick of life. Remember those who grieve the loss of loved ones, the loss of work, the loss of hope. Look in compassion on those who have lost their job and who now struggle with a sense of futility. O God, don't let us evade our own calling to address these troubles. Empower us to help.

Loving God, so many of us look at the world's trouble and find that darkness fills us and contaminates our faith. How can there be so much evil inside your providence? Shine in our darkness. Enlighten and reassure us. And hear the cries of your creatures, including your nonhuman creatures who suffer along with, and sometimes because of, us humans. Listen to your whole creation groan for deliverance. Hear all who cry to you, God of mercy.

As I hover at the edge of sleep, I entrust myself to your faithful keeping. *Amen.*

Morning

Lord Jesus Christ, this morning your blessed resurrection inspires all of us followers. The news of it is the heart of the gospel. And it straightens our spines. We can go around saying, "The Lord is risen," and we can expect to hear from other believers, "He is risen indeed."

To the desperate and bewildered we can say, "The Lord is risen." The same to doubters. The same to skeptics. To the poor people of the world who suffer first the indignity of their poverty and then the desolation of being blown out of their houses by hurricanes, or washed out by floods—all because they are too poor to build anything on habitable land—to these and so many others we can say that you are risen from the dead.

Your mighty resurrection isn't everything we have to offer the world by way of the gospel. But it's the platform of everything we have to offer. Every Christian hospital, college, orphanage, media ministry, counseling service, political party, relief agency, and AIDS clinic builds on this platform. Our hope rises with your resurrection because it tells us that your life-giving love cannot be defeated, not even by death.

Lord Jesus Christ,

> The house of my soul is small. Expand it.
> The house of my soul is dark. Illuminate it.

The house of my soul is lonely.
Enter and dwell in it forever.

Let the expanded house of my soul welcome guests who need to be there, and welcome you, whom I need to be there. Let the illuminated house of my soul expose my sins and dissolve them by the power of your purifying light. Let your indwelling of my soul fill me with joy and longing for the perfect union with you I hope for in the end.

All your people pray to you this morning. I join them to thank you for your incarnation, saving miracles, blessed teaching, atoning death, and glorious resurrection. You are our Lord. We trust you. *Amen.*

Evening

God of great might and weight, of great light and splendor, to you be glory for the things you have done. God who creates and saves, it is right and fitting always and everywhere to praise your greatness and to love your goodness.

With all your children I kneel before you. You know us all too well. You know both our silliness and our sadness. You know our littleness. You know how we have sinned.

I confess to you, O God, that we have often neglected our calling to serve others. We have ignored some who need us and have withheld the word of praise from others who hunger for it. Well fed and well loved, we have been too often full of ingratitude and self-pity. Forgive and heal us so that some part of your beauty may again come upon us.

Fountain of blessings, you fulfill needs we don't even know we have. You imagined each of us from all eternity, and one day breathed life into what you had imagined. You are present to us in joys and in sorrows, in sickness and in health.

Tonight, I want to thank you for all who have faithfully done their job today, and now rest. Thank you for

women and men who today inspected bridges,
　　cranes, and elevators,
police who patrolled streets and highways,
first responders who moved quickly
　　to the scenes of accidents,
9-1-1 operators who stayed calm
　　during frenzied calls, and
trustworthy child-care providers
　　who gave overworked parents relief.

Thank you for

wise counselors who listened attentively
　　to trouble,
early morning trash collectors who worked
　　almost silently,
airline pilots who concentrated
　　on their checklist,
moms and dads who hugged their children,
journalists who wrote honest accounts of events
　　they witnessed, and
business owners who treated employees
　　with respect.

I commend them all to you, O God, for your blessing, in Jesus's name. *Amen.*

Morning

To you, Lord Jesus Christ, is due all glory and renown. You bore our flesh. You taught us radical
love. You redeemed us from sin and shame. You chose
us to wear your name in the world. You will one day
give us a part in your new earthly reign. To you, Lord
Jesus Christ, is due all glory and renown.

This morning I celebrate your compassion. So
often, the Gospels tell us that you were moved by
someone's condition:

> "When you saw the leper . . ."
> "When you saw the blind man . . ."
> "When you saw the widow . . ."
> "When you saw the crowd looking harassed and
>   misled, like sheep without a shepherd . . ."

You never overlooked trouble. Never ignored it. You
saw it and were stirred by it. Then you followed through
and did something about it.

And you celebrated compassion in your stories. You
told us about a naked man, wounded and lying in the
road. A priest and a Levite passed him by, but a Samaritan, of all people, saw him, was moved to compassion,
and took care of him.

You told us about a father looking down the road,

26

hoping for a glimpse of his younger son. You told us that when he saw his prodigal son, he was moved by compassion and ran to him and embraced him and kissed him.

Lord Jesus Christ, Son of God, I want to follow you. Let me today see trouble and be moved by it. Let me today follow through with prayer or money or kind words or helpful actions. I know I'm not you. I know my compassion is finite and subject to fatigue. Rest and restore me, so that one day soon my compassion will be fresh and lively again.

I know I sometimes harden my heart. Soften it, Lord. Make my heart supple and responsive, so that, once more, I may be more like you, my teacher and savior. *Amen.*

Evening

Covenant God, your word of promise always establishes an island of certainty in a sea of uncertainty. Thank you that your word is sure and your promise dependable through Jesus Christ.

Eternally alert God, you know me. You search me and you know me.

> I can conceal my thoughts from others,
>> but not from you.
> I can hide my shame from others,
>> but not from you.
> I can outsmart my competitors,
>> but nobody outsmarts you.
> I can keep others in the dark, but not you,
>> because you have perfect night vision.

I am never out from under you. If I fly high, so do you. If I sink low, so do you. If I rise with the dawn or set with the evening sun, you rise and set right along with me. Up, down, east, west—never mind. No exit anywhere. I can't get outside you. You have no outdoors.

Vigilant God, I can't even retreat to the sanctuary of my own mind, because you track every thought. You record all the devices and desires of my heart. You know not only what I say but also what I think. You know not only what I say but also what I almost said. You know the kind word I forgot to say and the kind word I never dreamt of saying.

I have no escape, no retreat, no privacy at all. And so, tonight, I give up my anxiety about being watched. I give it up. And I surrender myself to your watchful presence. I know, deep down, that your knowledge of me is a loving knowledge. You wove me together in my mother's womb. You have not trapped me in a lab but cradled me in your grace.

Nobody else is up to the job of knowing me through and through and loving me still. My secrets are safe only with you.

O God, you hem me in behind and before. You lay your hands on me. Those loving, wounded hands. Hold me in them this very night. *Amen.**

* This prayer paraphrases Psalm 139.

Morning

God of promise, you brought your people out of the house of bondage and into the open space of freedom. You led them through the wilderness and into the promised land. I lift my voice this morning to sing and say your praise. Bring me, too, out from every bondage, every wilderness, so that my weary years may pass and my strong years may soon begin.

To you, loving God, I bring thanks for your abiding presence. In you I live and move and have my being.

> I rest in you.
> I nest in you.
> I am blessed in you.

In you, hospitable God, I find my heart's true home. I give you thanks for your abundant blessing and, above all, for your goodness on which I may feast, in Jesus's name.

Listening God, I speak to you this morning with simple trust. I depend on you for every good thing. And I speak as a member of Christ's body in the world. We all depend on you. We know you are not only good but also great. We know you can do strange and wonderful things. You can do miracles. Let us not be so skeptical that we fail to see them. But neither let us be so greedy for miraculous signs that we overlook the daily wonders of creation and providence all around us. They are impressive, but because they are so usual, we are not very impressed.

Give us, great God, open minds to seek your will, soft hearts to receive your will, and ready hands to do your will. We want to be weavers, O God. Teach us to weave together our work and witness into a seamless garment that warms others and that shows forth your beauty in the world.

We can't claim to be pure in our loyalty to you and to your Christ. We are too much the products of our culture and too little the products of your Holy Spirit. Have your way with us more and more. And, this day, O God, have your way with me, through Jesus Christ our Lord. *Amen.*

Evening

Gracious God, I am not naïve. I know that in the body of Christ faith abounds, but so does doubt.

> When children suffer, doubt arises.
> When animals suffer, doubt arises.
> When we pray and nothing happens,
>   doubt arises.
> When the wicked prosper and the righteous
>   wither, doubt arises.
> When we read certain parts of the Bible,
>   doubt arises.

Good God, I know this is nothing new. The Psalms are full of doubt. So were some of your biblical saints. What was behind your beloved Son's cry from the cross, asking why you had forsaken him?

Doubt doesn't surprise me. After all, the human mind is finite. Our spirits are willful. Our vision is clouded.

What surprises me is faith. Before I sleep tonight, I want to say to you how remarkable it is that so many of us believe. We can't help it. We didn't invent our faith, or engineer it, or whip it up. But there it is. Mysteriously, we have it. I know faith is our calling. But clearly it is also your gift.

I find myself believing the promises in your Word—that you have forgiven me, that you love me, that you forever have a place for me. I find myself trusting you to provide all that's needful for me. I have come to believe that it is safe to lean on you with all my weight, that you are my refuge and strength, a bulwark, a mighty stay within the shifting currents of life.

Generous God, none of this happens simply on my own. Part of your gift is that you have lodged me in a Christian community. Here I engage songs, prayers, Bible readings, preaching, sacraments, creeds, communion of saints—all these things expressing faith and strengthening my own. They expose me to the breathing of the Holy Spirit. Frankly accepting supernatural reality, my fellow believers openly defy secularists by practicing their faith, by rehearsing it. And, by your gift, I do too. In Jesus's name, *Amen.*

Morning

Steadfast God,

> The idols of the age are glitter and dust,
>   but you are my rock.
> The idols of the mind are appearance and
>   mirage, but you are my rock.
> The idols of the marketplace are in or out of
>   fashion, but you are my rock.
> The idols of this age collapse when people lean
>   on them, but you are my rock.

I have awakened to a new day and want to put this day in your hands. I want to

> think with your thinking,
> wish with your wishing, and
> strive with your striving.

Give me resonance, O God, with others around me. If my life feels like a song today, teach me to weep with those who weep. If today I feel strung tight or restless, walled in by loneliness or regret, bring me freedom to rejoice with all your children who rejoice.

I confess that I am often smudged by my failures and disheartened by my self-deception. I am unnerved

34

by circumstances I can't understand. Let your love lift me like a tide so that I float free of destructive pride and faithless fear. Float me out into the sea of your billowing love.

Make your way past the crowding of my little interests, and remind me today, tomorrow, and the next day in whose path I walk, to whose welcome I move, in whose promise I live and grow. For surely, O God, my own way is desolate, and my own house forsaken. My calendar is thick with things to rattle or undo me. I have no resources of my own for the coming hours. I'll not be strong enough, wise enough, or pure enough to keep from stumbling. And yet I'll be with you. So,

> let your strong arm save me,
> let the sound of your voice reassure me, and
> let the pattern of your ways direct me.

Surely, you are a God who comes to save through Jesus Christ. *Amen.*

Evening

Faithful God, as I approach the end of this day, I give myself into your safekeeping. You know me and love me. I am only one of billions who worship you, and yet you know my thoughts, my disposition, my character, my words and deeds—including the flaws in each of them. You know all these things and love me still. You know exactly who I am, and yet you love me.

I join my heart and voice to those of all your children. God of the nations, you bless the world through us. You elected Israel to be a blessing; you elected the church to be a blessing. Always you are out to bless, to adorn, to pour out value upon value. With praise and thanksgiving, we raise our song to you in Jesus's name.

O God, savior of the simple-hearted, you have heard us cry to you.

> You have preserved our lives so that
> > we have breath enough to praise you.
> You have preserved our wits so that
> > we have mind enough to thank you.
> You have preserved our hearts so that
> > we have ardor enough to love you.

You have done these things because of your goodness. Because of your sheer, overflowing goodness.

Rock of ages, make us strong and sure. God of streaming waters, make us clean and pure. God of towering trees and sweeping plains and rolling waves, you who touch our earth with beauty, touch our hearts and make them straight and true, through Jesus Christ our Lord.

Holy God, we belong to you, but we keep trying to belong to ourselves.

> Reach out to our confused minds
> and clear them.
> Reach out to our divided hearts
> and unite them.
> Reach out to our selfish intentions
> and humble them.

Reach out to all within us that is willful or wayward. Touch, restore, and heal till we are fully your own.

Have your own way with us, good God. Have your own way with me, too, and with all I love. In Jesus's name, *Amen.*

Morning

Everlasting God, send out your light and your truth. Let them lead me today. Your Son is the light of the world. Your Son is the way, the truth, and the life. Looking for Jesus, I want to find him. Looked for by Jesus, I want him to find me first.

Almighty God, nothing I do makes you seek me less; nothing I do makes you seek me more. You seek me with all the passion of a lover, and so I worship and adore you. Open me to your living presence today and in the days ahead, that you may create a river of joy in my heart from which I may overflow in thanks to you and in blessing to others.

Lay your blessing on me today.

> Enliven my faith.
> Raise my hope.
> Warm my love.

Let me help to make your name bigger in the world.

Today and in the coming days, stretch your sheltering tarp over me so that, under it, I may be safe from the pestilence that stalks in darkness and from all that would undo my faith. Let me be safe and secure in the knowledge of your undying love.

Saving God, I'm speaking to you as a member of the whole body of Christ. You led the wise by a star and brought them to Jesus. Put a star in our eyes today, that we too may come to Jesus in whom are hidden all the treasures of wisdom.

Lord Jesus Christ, Word of God incarnate, wisdom from on high, you mediated at creation, pouring your self-giving love into the world. You mediated in salvation, taking our flesh, taking our pain, taking the death we deserved. You mediate for us now in heaven. You have ascended on high for us and for our salvation. We thank and praise you.

Give us understanding, discernment, judgment of what's right. Give us your wisdom in great abundance. Let all of us today bring credit to you, with whom we live in blessed union. *Amen.*

Evening

Lord Jesus Christ, Son of God, you emptied yourself of heaven's riches and came to share our lot. You made yourself poor so that by your poverty we might become rich. Perfect in purity, you yet submitted to baptism like any sinner in need of cleansing.

So many tonight need your tender care. Tend to prisoners, caged and too often abandoned by family members. Tend to addicts, trapped by lethal hungers. Tend to prostitutes, used by the lust of strangers. Tend to refugees, who are footsore, threadbare, humiliated by their condition. Tend to the unemployed and underpaid, your lonely ones, your depressed ones, your wretched ones.

Wear your look of welcome for sisters and brothers whose calling this night is to die. Escort them by a party of angels into your radiance and light them up with the rays of your love. Tell them that their sins have been forgiven, and that they are now blanketed in your righteousness. Promise them a future filled with love and joy.

Suffering Son of God, our minds do not grasp the length and breadth, the height and depth, of your love for us sinners and for our world, which is gripped by the power of sin. Our minds do not grasp your unfathom-able love, but our hearts hold it. Our hearts do hold it.

Exalted Son of God, I have my loved ones much on my mind tonight. I'm thinking of _____ and of _____ and of _____.

> Go before them to lead them.
> Go behind them to guard them.
> Go beneath them to support them.
> Go beside them to befriend them.

Do not let them be afraid. Extract their fear and re-place it with your peace. Let your blessing fall on them tonight and settle in around them. Do not let them be afraid.

Soon it will be time for me to quiet my thoughts and to fall away into slumber. Please push away the fright-ening dreams, and bring forward the sweet ones, so that I may sleep under the arch of your blessing. Tomorrow, let me awaken refreshed and ready for a new day. In Jesus's name, *Amen.*

Morning

God of grace and God of glory, at the threshold of this day, I lift my heart to you, whose giving knows no end. You offer riches I can no more measure than deserve. Sun and stars are yours to give. Heaven and earth are yours to give. The *new* heaven and earth are yours to give. I lift my heart to you whose giving knows no end.

> If my heart is hesitant, make it bold.
> If my heart is afraid, make it confident.
> If my heart is listless, make it stout.

I want to be generous, just as you are. Make me openhanded, O God,

> not only with my money
>   but also with my time,
> not only with my time
>   but also with my attention,
> not only with my attention
>   but also with my encouragement.

You are lavish with your goodness poured out on sinners. Let this be my model, my example, my inspiration. Let me learn to spend myself, and in self-spending to find my fulfillment.

Today let me be generous in my assessment of others. Let me not face them with a cynical mind. Let me give them the benefit of the doubt. Let me try to put the best face on their motives and acts. If a person does something right, let me say, "That's who she is." If she does something wrong, let me say, "I'm surprised."

O God, because your holy Word so often pleads for the poor, let me be especially generous with them. Let me be slow to blame them for their poverty and quick to bless them with some of what I have from you. Let me be quick to note that some of them are generous too. I know what I have is from you. All good things are. I'm just a spreader of your good gifts, and I want to be an openhanded one.

Blessed God, it's the start of a new day. Let me be generous in it, through Jesus Christ. *Amen.*

Evening

L oving God, you are worthy of praise in a thousand tongues. Let English and French tongues praise you tonight. Let Dutch and Hungarian tongues praise you. Let Israeli and Palestinian tongues praise you. Let Brazilian and Honduran tongues praise you. Let Chinese and Korean tongues praise you. Let all people on earth praise you and magnify your name in their own language.

Before I go to sleep, I want to assess how I acted today.

> Have I blamed the needy or helped them?
> Have I felt blessed or entitled?
> Have I been willing to be obscure,
>   or have I tried to be noticed?
> Have I been grateful for your gifts to others,
>   or have I resented them?
> Have I been diligent today or lazy?

You know how tempted I am to fool myself, but tonight let my self-assessment be straight and true.

Forgiving God, remove today's sins from me and scatter them in the wind. Remove the taint I bear for involvement in the world's corporate sin. Blow these things away. Abolish them, reject them, banish them. And, please, take whatever I did that was right today and build it into me. Build it in, work it in, iron it in so that it becomes part of my character and eventually part of my destiny. I know my good works can't save me. But I don't want to be without them, either.

As a member of the church of Christ, I appeal to you now. Send your Holy Spirit to quicken us.

> Forgive us by your grace.
> Instruct us by your truth.
> Relieve us by your mercy.

Holy Father, you created the world through your mediating Son and brooding Spirit. Lord Jesus Christ, on the Father's mission you redeemed the world your Father loves. Holy Spirit of Father and Son, you blew power into the church and sent her out to the world.

Majestic God, triune from all ages, brimming with life upon life in triplicate verve, you poured out loving power to create, save, and inspire. We adore you through Jesus Christ. *Amen.*

Morning

Great God, redeemer of the lost and blind, you so often cut through the armor of cruel men. You get them in the heart and save them. You saved John Newton, a slaver. You got him in the heart so acutely that he grieved over his sins. He grieved over his sins so deeply that what poured from him was a song of amazing grace. He was lost, but you found him. He was blind, but you healed him. He had come through many dangers, toils, and snares, but you led him home through Jesus Christ.*

Compassionate God, this morning I lift to you so many others who grieve. Somewhere today a wife will get injured and a husband will die. Somewhere today a plant will close, and people will lose their jobs. Somewhere today a faithful mom will lament that her children have turned their backs on her. Somewhere a child will live a lie for fear her parents will turn their backs on her on account of the one she loves. Gracious God, if I go online, I see grief everywhere. People grieving over their poverty, over the diminishments of aging, over their poor judgment that led to a tragic mistake, over fam-

---

* See "Amazing Grace," #691, in *Lift Up Your Hearts: Psalms, Hymns, and Spiritual Songs* (Grand Rapids: Faith Alive, 2013).

ily estrangements, including bad marriage and divorce. People who, like John Newton, grieve over their sins.

If I add trouble in church, trouble in politics, trouble with neighborhood bigotry, trouble in a bitterly divided nation, I meet a mountain of grief. And people having trouble getting over it. I see people grieving over the loss of their faith, too. Somewhere today, people will grieve that their distress has knocked out their faith. They've simply seen too much trouble, and it has obscured their vision of you.

Restore them, O God. Make yourself large and unmistakable to them. Make yourself too big to miss. Loving God, the grieving need you.

> Comfort them.
> Accompany them.
> Bless and keep them.

To the extent that any of the rest of us can be a help, use us. Use us to express honest sympathy. Use our prayers, use our good wishes, use whatever may tend to help.

Attentive God, you know my own grief, and you will get to it. But this morning, please get to others first. In Jesus's name, *Amen.*

Evening

Eternal God, mighty in the heavens, you brought back from the dead our Lord Jesus Christ, lifting him to life and drawing him up into the glory he shares with you and the Holy Spirit. Stretch my mind and heart toward your great stature and majestic love. Raise my eyes, lift my head, expand my vision of you and your sovereign purposes in the world.

Pentecostal God, I join my voice with those of believers across the world. Pour out your Spirit on us. God of rushing wind, coming from where it wants and going to where it wants, pour out your Spirit on us. God of fire, flaring on gathered disciples and burning away their stubborn pride, pour out your Spirit on us. God of miraculous speaking and hearing, amazing the faithful and riveting their attention, pour out your Spirit on us.

You are the God of the young who see visions, of the old who dream dreams, of young prophets and old prophets, male prophets and female prophets.

> You are God of wonders above and signs below.
> You are God of blood and fire
>   and billowing smoke.
> You are God of blackened sun
>   and bloodied moon.

You raised up Peter to prophesy at Pentecost, to preach straight truth to a crooked generation, to accuse his own people of complicity in the death of Jesus. You used Peter's preaching to stab people in the heart with your grace and save them.

> God of wind and fire and tongues,
> God of visions and dreams and prophecies,
> God of signs and wonders, of blood and fire,
> pour out your Spirit on us.

This very night, good God, pour out your Spirit on me.

> My heart is too often hard. Soften it.
> My attention is too often wayward. Focus it.
> My will is too often bent. Straighten it.

Soften, focus, straighten so that I may conform my life to your will and help to sharpen your profile in the world.

O God, let your reputation become larger and more lustrous. Let people hear your name and rejoice in it. Let people turn their faces toward you so that you may shine on them. In Jesus's name, *Amen.*

Morning

O God, we human beings try so hard to secure ourselves. We wire our houses, lock our doors, change our passwords. We insure our lives, insure our health, insure our possessions. We invest in securities. We stockpile weapons. But then a report comes back from a pathology lab, and we know that life itself has never been entirely secure. Strong God, you are our only fortress.

I lift to you those who especially need security. I lift to you those who today will feel the lash of racism. Someone will make a remark, or give them a look, or take an action that clearly excludes them. Each of them is made in your own image, but racists think that's not good enough. Each is precious in your sight, but to bigots that's not good enough. Each of these brothers and sisters is as good as anyone else, but somehow that's still not good enough. They may be highly accomplished in law, or business, or education, or church life, but are not regarded as equal partners. With all their hurt and bewilderment and frustration, they need a place to go, gracious God. Be their fortress.

I lift to you those who today will feel the sting of sexism. They will earn less pay for equal work. Their judgment will be suspected, their achievements diminished, their hopes dismissed. Each of them is made in your own image, but sexists think that's not good enough. Each is precious in your sight, but to bigots that's not good enough. Their husbands will demand obedience. So will their fathers, even after they have grown up. They may be highly accomplished in law, or business, or education, or church life, but are not regarded as equal partners. With all their hurt and bewilderment and frustration, they need a place to go, gracious God. Be their fortress.

I lift to you all those who today will feel the scourge of bias against sexual minorities. They did not choose their orientation. They discovered it. And yet they are excluded, insulted, reviled. Each of them is made in your own image, but biased people think that's not good enough. Each is precious in your sight, but to bigots that's not good enough. Blocked at work, shunned by a part of society, cold-shouldered even at church, they feel the disapproval aimed at them. They may be highly accomplished in law, or business, or education, or church life, but are not regarded as equal partners. With all their hurt, all their bewilderment, all their frustration, they need a place to go, gracious God. Be their fortress.

Forgive us all for our involvement in structural racism, sexism, and bias against sexual minorities.

O God, you alone are our fortress, through Jesus Christ. *Amen.*

Evening

God of all, your children are prone to pride or despair. Some of us look on our lives with pleasure. We may have suffered in adolescence, but now we have risen. We own sleek cars and sizeable houses. Or we have earned many degrees. Our bodies have been fixed and slimmed. Our bank accounts have been opened and fattened. In your providence, some of us have married well. All our children are above average. To tell the truth, O God, we look around us and feel mighty satisfied with where we are.

Correct us, good God, and give us wisdom. Remind us that power and esteem and intellectual sophistication and middle-class comfort and the starring roles of our children—none of this can save us or forgive us or make us whole. Only your compassion for us foolish people can do these things. Your compassion and the dying and rising of Jesus.

Against all temptations to pride, remind us how little we have that is safe and how little we have that is ours.

Lord God, some of us look on our lives with a much darker spirit. We have failed to go far. People don't often remember us. We have to reintroduce ourselves way too often. We are lightweights in our own eyes. We have second mortgages or second spouses or second thoughts about ourselves. Our careers have slowly fizzled. Our brains have gone soft from junk food. Our children are sometimes boring even to us.

Loving God, remind us how little of this finally matters. None of it can condemn us in your eyes. None of it can make us little or loveless. Against all temptation to despair, secure us with your persistent mercy that comes to lift and to embrace and to make us strong.

Then gift us with faith in your love. Nothing we do can make you love us more. Nothing we do can make you love us less. You have this marvelous enthusiasm for us that keeps us from swinging away from you. It's your love, always your love, only your love that can steady our wobbly lives. In Jesus's name, *Amen.*

Morning

Steadfast God, I add my voice to the great choir of witnesses in heaven and on earth. God of our future, you have promised a new heaven and earth. Your peace is before us. God of our past, you made peace through Jesus's blood shed on the cross. Your peace is behind us. God of our hearts, you forgive our worst and summon our best. Your peace is within us. Bless us, and keep us, and cause your face to shine on us, and grant us your peace always.*

God of lively energy, I don't want to be lazy today. You know I've been lazy often enough before. I have resisted work, resented work, detoured around work, obsessed over work *while avoiding it*, and so have turned work into something twice as unpleasant as it would have been if I had simply tackled it.

Merciful God, this is stupid, and I don't want anything to do with it.

I know my fellow believers are going to be busy today. They're going to ask, seek, and knock, and I want to join them. They're going to let their light shine, and I want to join them. They're going to do good for others, and I want to do it, too. They're going to seek your kingdom first, and I want to seek it alongside them.

* Numbers 6:24–26.

I can't do any of this from my recliner.

Good God, your people are going to be busy today. They'll fight fires, fix teeth, lay carpet, write sermons, repair cars, chase news stories, teach kids, husband animals, farm the good earth, and struggle to get a widow's case to court before her witnesses go stale. In their own way, all these things contribute to your kingdom of shalom. All are for flourishing. And I can't be part of them if I am lazy.

God of burning energy, give me ambition today— holy ambition, noble ambition, kingdom ambition. You are going to be working today, and I am ambitious to join your work. As far as you give me energy and direction, I want to be part of the action. In Jesus's name, *Amen.*

Evening

God of the prophets, you love mercy and justice. You love them both, even when they seem in tension. You showed that you love them both in the life and death of your beloved Son, who was obedient to law, who suffered the penalty we deserved, and who won mercy for us sinners. Your mercy and your justice have become my song.

O God, it's evening and time to lay aside today's work. So many of us got busy today with good things to do. So many of us tonight are a little weary. Give us rest, O God. Our days are heavy with obligations, and our nights disturbed by worries over them. Give us rest, O God. We are tired of battling old temptations and besetting sins, battling structural sin and national idolatries, tired by our defeats and tired from despairing over them. Give us rest, O God. We are tired from trying to fix people who won't get fixed and don't want us to try anymore. Give us rest, O God, and give them rest, too.

Eternal Father of our Lord Jesus Christ, who welcomed into his easy yoke all who are weary and burdened, our hearts are restless until they come to rest in you. In you, infinite God, we find our firm foundation and our everlasting security. You have been our dwelling place throughout all generations. Before the mountains were born, or you brought forth the whole world, from everlasting to everlasting, you are God.

We are only mortals, creatures of dust who return to dust. In the morning you wake us up into the thunder of life. In the evening you sweep us away in the sleep of death. We are only mortals, mere transients in the world. Our days quickly pass, and we fly away. Our times are in your hands, because from everlasting to everlasting you are God. Teach us to number our days, that we may gain a heart of wisdom.*

I rest tonight in the cocoon of your gentle care. I entrust myself to you, gracious God, through Jesus Christ. *Amen.*

---

* This and the previous paragraph paraphrase Psalm 90.

Morning

Yours is the night, great God, for the moon to beam. Yours is the day, O God, for the sun to shine. Yours is the night, yours is the day, yours is the light upon my way. All yours, always yours, only yours.

Today, O God, I intercede for all of us human beings, that you may wipe out some of our folly. We smoke, or drink, or eat, or self-medicate into addictions. The addiction causes us distress. Then we try to relieve the distress with the same thing that caused it. We trap ourselves, O God, and need you to set us free.

Some of us won't listen. Nobody can teach us anything. Some of us give the world an irritable attitude, a sharp tongue, a haughty spirit. Some of us lie and cheat. Good God, this is folly. It's wrong, but it's also stupid because it aborts the very possibility of real fellowship. And that's a blessing we should not miss. In your mercy, remove our folly.

O God, sometimes we deny you, or turn away from you, or spurn your love. We fail to honor and thank you. In other words, we unplug our own ventilator. Good God, this is folly. In your mercy, abolish it.

All our sinning is folly, O God. I know it and confess it. I know sin is

the wrong recipe for good health,
the wrong fuel for the human motor, and
the wrong road to get home.

When we go to our idols, great God, we become
not only treacherous but also foolish. We fascinate ourselves with the currently popular idols of this world,
and then find that they can't deliver. They can't forgive
us, accept us, improve us. They can't ever save us. If we
try to fill ourselves with anything but you, we find that
we are overfed but undernourished and that, day by
day, we are thinning down to a mere silhouette of a
human being.

In your mercy, O God, destroy some of our folly
today. It will be holy work in Jesus's name. *Amen.*

Evening

God of grace and God of glory, your people sing to you tonight with all our hearts.

> You make and keep us.
> You shelter and defend us.
> You forgive and renew us.

Your mercies are tender and firm to the end.

Creator God, you spoke worlds into being. Let the angels praise you. Your name alone is high. Let the hosts of heaven praise you. Your glory is exalted. Let sun and moon and stars all praise you in Jesus's name.

Mighty God, we have no words adequate to acclaim your greatness. So, let the horns flare and the violins sing to praise you. We stammer in trying to speak of your majesty. So, let the cymbals ring and the drums beat to praise you. Let dancers stretch and leap and bend to praise you. Let signers move their eyes and mouths and hands to praise you.

From you comes every grace that pardons and lifts. Do pardon our sin through Jesus Christ, our Lord. Do lift our souls to you, great giver of life and health. Remember, good Lord, your love for us. In our mind's eye, let us see all those you have pardoned and lifted, and let the sight strengthen and inspire us.

Mighty and loving God, you wrestled with Jacob till his magnificent defeat. Wrestle with us too. You straightened a crooked man. Straighten us too. You are the God of Jacob. You are forever our God, too.

Loving God, tonight I thank you for all who have faithfully done their job today, and now rest. Thank you for the men and women who today cut hair, set bones, and taught math to middle schoolers. Thank you for those who today fought corruption, buried the dead, encouraged the weak. Some today manufactured useful goods, or delivered them, or stocked and sold them. Thank you for them all. Some drove a bus. Some designed a house. Some laid tile, installed a sink, fixed a leaky roof. Some evangelized the lost. Others were neighborly to people on their street. I commend them all to you, O God, for blessing in Jesus's name. They did their job. And now they get to rest. *Amen.*

Morning

Great God, make this a bad day for tyrants. Unseat and scatter them. Replace them with righteous rulers. Vindicate the oppressed. Crown them with glory and honor. Let their children silence foes and avengers by singing your praise.*

At the start of this new day, O God, I lament all the cheating in the world. Cheaters seem to have their way. Some of them prosper. They cheat on their spouses and taxes. They cheat their workers and suppliers. Some workers cheat their employers out of an honest day's work for an honest day's pay. People cheat themselves out of any chance at real intimacy just by being arrogant. People cheat even when they're trying to have fun. They cheat at golf and cheat at cards and cheat at tennis. Great and honest God, all this cheating is irritating and depressing.

I lament all the lying in the world. Friends lie to each other; children and parents lie to each other; husbands and wives, brothers and sisters lie to each other. Motorists lie to cops; presidents of countries lie to their people. Advertisers lie to consumers, airline companies to passengers, attorneys to clients, and clients to attorneys. Representatives and senators lie to citizens. Patients lie

* The last two sentences paraphrase Psalm 8:5, 2.

to doctors about their drinking and smoking. We lie in our rebukes and in our compliments. Our facial expressions lie. Our body language lies. We lie about our lies. We lie even to ourselves. Great and honest God, all this lying is hurtful and depressing.

But I'm going to have to confess to you that I have lied and cheated too. It's not just others. It's me, too. O God, forgive me. Search me and know me, but don't stop loving me. Make me a lover of truth, a lover of simple justice.

As I go about my business today, guard my mouth and guide my hands. Let me be straight with people and let them be straight with me. Let me live today in such a way that on your great day of judgment I can look back on *this* day and not be ashamed, under the cloak of Jesus's righteousness. *Amen.*

Evening

God of all providence, in Jesus Christ you give living water for the thirsty, bread of life for the hungry, the shelter of your wings for the fearful. Lord Jesus Christ, Son of God, thank you for your mercy.

> Dim in knowledge, I call to you.
> > Christ, be my light.
> Cold of heart, I cry to you.
> > Christ, be my warmth.
> Unsure at crossroads, I appeal to you.
> > Christ, be my guide.

Shine through the darkness. Always my light, my warmth, my guide.

Loving God, father of Jesus, I pray today for the lost and hopeless. Your kingdom come. Remember the despised and trampled. Your kingdom come. Bend your ear toward all who cry to you. Your kingdom come. Your will be done on earth as it is in heaven.

Some of us do see signs, O God. We see signs that one day your kingdom will come in its fullness. We see in epidemics that doctors and nurses risk their lives to heal the sick. Lovers of justice rescue innocent convicts and thus inspire other lovers of justice. Your Spirit penetrates hard hearts and makes them tender toward you and toward others. Thank you, generous God. We do see signs that point to your glory.

Lover of the world to whom you sent your Son, I confess to you that I have not gone out to the world you love.

> I have sought comfort more than compassion.
> I have loved entertainment more than outreach.
> I have loved hunkering down more than looking
> up to your standard of justice.

Chasten me so that I may become a more profitable servant.

Loving God, two billion of us Christians today need your healing touch. Touch the wounds in the body of Christ. Quiet our strife, repair our divisions. Unite us by your word and Spirit. Let us walk together in the joy of Christ your Son.

O God, so much of life is a din. So much of life is a rush. Invite us to be still and know that you are God, through Jesus Christ. *Amen.*

Morning

Creator God, at the outset of this new day I turn my eye to what you have made. You are the redeeming God, but before that you are the creating God. You redeem only what's already there, the product of your imagination and work and love of beauty.

Job tells us that you revel in your creation.*

> You walk in the depths of the sea.
> You cut water channels through deserts.
> You lead bear cubs out of their dens.
> You make a pet of Leviathan.
> You provide a nightly crib for wild oxen.
> You father the rain and mother the ice.

At the dawn of time, angels and stars formed an audience and then a choir as they watched you at work on creation. You laid the foundation of the earth "while the morning stars sang together / and all the angels shouted for joy."**

O God, all this makes my spine tingle. Your good creation excites my senses. I love its sights—the way distant mountains can look bluish-purple and the way

* E.g., chapters 38 and 39.
** Job 38:7 NIV 2011.

66

an ocean seen from a cliff can look impossibly vast. So much to watch—seagulls riding air currents, Labrador retrievers plunging into a pond to fetch a ball, cumulus clouds drifting across a blue, blue sky.

I love the sounds of nature—singing birds, rustling leaves, crashing waves, croaking frogs, babbling brooks. I love the smells of moistened earth, of peonies and phlox and lilac, of campfires and cut cedar and fresh ozone.

I love the taste of so many things you've made—of ripe apples and sweet plums, of bell peppers and grilled asparagus and black sweet cherries. I love the feel of a baby's brow and a puppy's coat, of a satin dress and my beloved's skin.

God of beauty, I know that creation now groans under its burden of decay and exploitation. But I also know that you will one day make all things new. Meanwhile, what delights my senses also tantalizes me with the promise of the new creation. Thank you in Jesus's name. *Amen.*

Evening

Bountiful God, who reached for me with a hand of mercy, thank you for your unfailing love. You hate sin but you love sinners, and so you are always out to save. "You did not send your Son into the world to condemn the world, but so that the world might be saved, through him."* You are good to the world, you are good to the church, and you are good to me, in Jesus's mighty name. Thank you.

I add my voice tonight to those of all your thankful people. With you, wonderful God, we enjoy peace through our Lord Jesus Christ. You have pardoned us through his precious blood. You have erased our sin. You have made our spirits whole. You have given us a resting place inside your love. Thank you.

Wonderful God, you are an overflowing fountain of mercy.

> You comfort the sorrowing
> with your plenteous love.
> You lift the weak
> with your boundless strength.
> You guide the erring
> with your abundant wisdom.

* See John 3:17.

Our own lives are like grass that withers or like flowers that fade.* But your love is from everlasting to everlasting. Thank you.

Life can be full of dark, dark places, but I'm not looking there tonight. I'm looking into the full sun of your bounty. And there I find so much goodness. You bless human beings with great talent for music and art, so that when their work is in our lives, we ache at the beauty of it. You bless human beings with great talent for telling stories that ring true. You give storytellers to imagine a whole world, and we get to dwell in their world. We love it so much that, when the story ends and we must step outside their world, we feel like weeping. Thank you.

Lord God, master of the universe, from you comes all that makes us grow. You feed us with your word. You satisfy us with wisdom from on high. We give you thanks through Jesus Christ, our Lord. *Amen.*

* Isaiah 40:8.

Morning

G od of wonder, God of might, your whole creation
shimmers with beauty.

> You made surging oceans and running streams.
> You grew forest trees and filled them
>   with singing birds.
> You crowned human beings
>   with glory and honor.
> By the mouths of infants,
>   you silenced the foe and the avenger.*
> You elected Israel to be a blessing to all nations.
> In the fullness of time,
>   you sent Jesus to save the world you love.

Great God, beauty so old, so new, so high, so near,
I worship you.

In this new day, I tune my voice to sing your praise
for the wonder of my baptism. You have set your sign
on me. In baptism you marked me as belonging to your
people across the ages and across the world. You gave
me the mark of belonging to Christ the king. He pur-
sued his strong life, suffered his terrible death, launched
his glorious coming-to-life, and now you have made

---

* The last two sentences paraphrase Psalm 8:5, 2.

these events my events because you have made me a living member of the people formed by these events. You have moved me inside the sphere of your blessing, so that songs and sermons and sacraments and wise people would all exert force to nudge me toward the center where Jesus dwells. Today, as I remember my baptism, my heart fills with gratitude to you because you have set your sign on me.

Triune God, great beating heart of the universe, you have drawn me to your wonder. In your burning purity, you have drawn me to your holiness. In your self-spending love for sinners, you have drawn me to your goodness.

Our suffering world needs you today. To the victims of war, O God, bring shalom. To migrants bring food and shelter. Disarm terrorists. Restrain lovers of war. Raise up great and calm statesmanship in the world. Multiply peacemakers. Teach us to love our own enemies, forgiving them, reimagining them, even if it takes a long time and so much of your favor.

Today, O God, I want to follow Jesus. *Amen.*

Evening

O God, your people give you hearty thanks for your matchless grace.

> While we were still sinners, you loved us.
> While we were still strangers, you welcomed us.
> While we were still enemies, you befriended us.

We have ignored and grieved you, but you have freely forgiven us. Beyond all reasoning, beyond all deserving, beyond all human imagining, you have forgiven us through the sacrificial work of Jesus Christ your Son.

Rescuer of the shamed, you reach into human pits to lift the fallen.

> We sink into addiction,
>   and you come to heal.
> We sink into folly,
>   and you come to correct.
> We sink into corruption,
>   and you come to sanctify.

Refuge of all who suffer, we look for shelter in the shadow of your wings. Rain and hail and wind beat on your wings, but they do not fold. They are spread out like Jesus's arms on the cross, spread out to protect all who seek shelter beneath them.

Architect of mysteries, you had Moses raise the serpent up to cure snakebite. You arranged the world so that whoever believes in your Son, lifted on the cross, will not perish but have everlasting life.* In your mercy, his death is the antivenom that prevents our death. Mysterious God, your ways are higher than our ways.

O God, wondrous in love for sinners, we give you thanks for your saving grace. You do not hold against us our treachery and neglect but let them drop. You do not hold against us our conceit and indifference but let them go. Forgiveness is your gift to us. Even our faith is your gift. We have been saved by grace through faith—and all this is your gift. Surely there is none like you. Spread your protective wings over me as I sleep. In Jesus's name, *Amen.*

---

* John 3:14.

Morning

To you, holy God, I lift my heart at the outset of this day, trusting your faithfulness and looking for opportunities you may open before me. You have always been good to me beyond my deserving. You have never led me wrong. Today, I want to be in your hands and at your disposal. If I should meet someone today who is wounded, let me show mercy. If guilty, let me offer forgiveness. If depressed, let me give encouragement.

Let me become a little wiser today. Let me know your creation—its boundaries and limits, its laws and rhythms, its times and seasons. I want to understand today that I am going to reap what I sow. Let me know that you are my superior, that other human beings are my peers, that nonhuman creation has its own integrity that I am blessed to accept. Let me fit myself into your setup.

Today, good God, I want to believe that to spend myself is the way to thrive, that to flourish I must help others to flourish.

Help me today to be discerning. Let me see the difference between pleasure and joy and between sentimentality and compassion. Let me see that facts are stubborn things and that I shouldn't try to finesse them to suit my own wishes. Good God, I need wisdom. I need to understand deep down that the more I talk, the less people will listen; that if my word is no good, people will not trust me; that if I refuse to work hard and take pains, I am unlikely to do much of any consequence; that boasting of my accomplishments does not make people admire them.

Help me today to understand that many valuable things, including happiness and deep sleep, come to me only if I do not try hard for them. Give me wisdom, O God. Let me commit not only to your Son but also to his program for living in the world. Let me understand that self-expenditure leads finally not to depletion but to abundant life.

I give myself to you today. In Jesus's name I pray, *Amen.*

Evening

Wonderful God, your power that raised Jesus from the dead is at work in me. You can do not only what I ask but also what I imagine; not only what I ask or imagine but far more than I ask or imagine. You can do *abundantly* far more than I ask or imagine. How wide, how long, how high, how deep is your love.*

Without it we are jittery people. Looking at our own success in life, we oscillate between pride and despair. Sometimes we think we've made it, and sometimes we think we'll never make it. But when your love flows to us like a river, we find rest, we find repose, we find peace at last.

I trust you. Lover of sinners,

> you seek out the lost to find them,
> you seek out the blind to heal them, and
> you seek out the bound to free them.

Liberator of slaves to sin, we need you every hour. We are addicted to the praise of people just as hapless as we are. We are bound by desires that keep doubling and tripling. But in Jesus Christ you have come to set us free.

* Ephesians 3:20, 18.

76

The evening is deepening. The sun is sinking, and the shadows are lengthening. I am going to entrust my body and spirit to rest in your care. But, before I do, I appeal to you, merciful God, for the world's troubled ones. They are grieving losses almost greater than they can bear. They are trapped by poverty. They are anxious, depressed, uncertain. Be their mercy tonight. Eternal refuge of the troubled, comfort, lift, and steady them.

> Though waters roar and foam, I will be still
>   and know that you are God.
> Though mountains quake, I will be still.
> Though nations roar, I will be still.
> Though terrorists scheme, I will be still
>   and know that you are God.* *Amen.*

* Psalm 46:2, 3, 6, 10.

Morning

Holy Spirit of God, you bring light and splendor. Dawn on my soul. You kindle joy and love. Glow within my spirit. You are alive with the power of God. Dwell in my heart.

Lord Jesus Christ, you emptied yourself of the riches of heaven to enter our life and become a servant. Let me learn some humility from you. The real thing. Not some counterfeit I use to fish for praise. Not a ploy to manipulate others into doing what I want.

Let me walk in the world today conscious of my place in the scheme of things. I am not a sovereign. I am your follower and a child of God your Father. I am not elevated above others. I am their peer, colleague, sibling, equal.*

Master, I want to be realistic about my status in the world. I want to have my two feet on the ground, to be down-to-earth. Let me today look out on the world sanely and sensibly. I want no fantasies of my superiority. I don't want to put on airs. Let me be grounded in sheer reality. Let those I encounter today meet not a prima donna but a fellow traveler. Let me respect them,

* I owe several thoughts in this prayer to Robert C. Roberts, *Spiritual Emotions: A Psychology of Christian Virtues* (Grand Rapids: Eerdmans, 2007), 78–93.

uphold them, fellowship with them. Let me take a genuine interest in them.

But in my enthusiasm for humility today, don't let me lurch over toward humiliation. You took on the form of a servant, not the form of a doormat. You didn't do everything people wanted you to do. You didn't cringe or grovel. You spoke sharply to hypocrites. So, too, let me not offer people submission when what they really need from me is resistance. I'm not their superior, but neither am I their inferior. Give me a quiet confidence in my own abilities and worth, knowing they are from you. So, let me look on these gifts less with pride than with gratitude.

Good Lord, I am going to try to walk through this day in real humility. I will have a chance only if you walk with me. *Amen.*

Evening

To you, loving God, I lift my heart, knowing that you are never further than the reach of my need and my prayer. You are God alone. None of your competitors matches up. None of our idols stands a chance. You alone know all, can do all, can be everywhere. You alone are as great in love as you are in power.

Have mercy on us. We are so often footloose in the earth, wandering from you, wandering from your people, wandering even from our own best interests. But you are the one that calls us back from our wanderings, reaching to us in our silence and in our tumult, calling us to our heart's true home.

Compassionate God, full of mercy for the wounded, your people speak to you from hearts that should be full of sorrow. We have sins that everybody knows, and they should be our sorrow. We have sins that nobody knows, and they should be our sorrow:

> old sins, new sins, sins upon sins
> sins of our youth, sins of our middle age,
>   sins of our old age
> individual sins, communal sins, private sins,
>   public sins

We have always more sins than we count or want to confess.

Now, for this moment at least, they are our sorrow. Our assurance, compassionate God, is that earth has no sorrows that heaven cannot heal.

Thank you, good God, for those who have faithfully done their jobs today.

> Truckers who hauled essential goods
> > to their destinations.
> Hairdressers who styled wigs
> > for cancer patients.
> Aides who performed patient,
> > steady work in nursing homes.
> Trainers who prepared guide dogs
> > to help the people who need them.
> Language interpreters who connected doctors
> > with patients in hospitals.

O God, they did their work today and now look to rest from it.

It's time for me to rest, too. Let me recline tonight in the sure knowledge of your love. In Jesus's name, *Amen.*

Morning

Loving God, you gave the righteousness of Christ to cover us. You wanted to warm us in a world grown chilly from our sin. You wanted to remove our sins from view, to clothe our nakedness, to ease our shame, to celebrate us as your beloved people. We give you hearty thanks.

Thank you for waking me to a new day. I want today to love my neighbor as myself. It's your command, and I know it's good for my neighbor and good for me. I'll need your gift of love flowing through me today, and I'll need my own determination to let it flow and to direct it toward those who need it.

How can I love my neighbor as myself today? Let me see my neighbor as your child, created in your image. Even when he's irritating. Even when she's unfair. Underneath everything, let me see your child, born of your imagination and love.

Let me today avoid especially one sin against my neighbor. Block me today from being judgmental. I know myself, O God. I know I can criticize someone in a tone of voice that suggests moral failure on their part and moral success on mine. Please stop this in me today. I don't want to sound self-righteous, and I don't want to be self-righteous.

I don't want to be hasty in my judgments, either. Block any that are. Let my assessment of my neighbor wait a while. Let me hear her story first. Let me consider her challenges. Let me weep and pray with her for a time. Let my judgments wait.

Finally, good God, I don't want to presume in my judgments today. I don't know my neighbor's inner life. I can't see how he's wired. I can't tell exactly what drives him. So, I can't presume to judge how blameworthy he is. I just don't know. I need to leave those judgments to you.

Let me love you above all today. And, especially in the judgment department, let me love my neighbor as myself. In Jesus's name, *Amen.*

Evening

Loving God, defender of the weak and rescuer of the lost—you saved me. I was cast down and you raised me up. I was at loose ends and you knitted me whole. I was a stranger and you befriended me.

You have cinched your people into union with Jesus Christ your Son.

> Nobody can break this bond.
> Nobody can pry us apart.
> Nothing can tear us from our Savior's grasp.

Great God, spinner of galaxies, you love us.

> You greet us with words of welcome.
> You nourish us with good food.
> You embrace us as your own.

We are your children, and you treat us as belonging to you.

Throughout history your people have cried to you in their distress. They were in bondage, and they cried to you. They were wandering in the wilderness, and they cried to you. They were desolate in exile, and they cried to you. We cry to you now for all the slaves in the world, for all the wanderers, for all who are exiled from home. Remember your mercy in these trying days.

Lord Jesus Christ, comforter of the weary, give us rest. We are sick and tired, and sick and tired of being sick and tired. Give us rest. We have worn ourselves out on trivial things and exhausted ourselves with perishing things.

Lord Jesus Christ, savior of the nations, you were willing to suffer that we might be healed. You did not hold yourself aloof from human misery but took the worst of it to yourself. You did not let the cup of sorrow pass but drank it down. We give you humble thanks that you did all this for us, your weary ones.

You who have triumphed over the shades of night, rise above our shadowed lives. Rise above our doubts. Rise above our sorrows. Rise above every bad memory and crumbling hope. Sun of righteousness, arise, and make your resurrection the magnet for ours.

Before I go to sleep, I give myself into your keeping. *Amen.*

Morning

To you, wonderful God, I lift my heart at the outset of this day, confident of your tender mercies.

> You seek and save me.
> You have and hold me.
> You plan good things for me.

I want to trust you today. After all, you are the one who acts with might in history. You led your people out of bondage in Egypt, out of the wilderness, out of exile. You sent your Son in the flesh and made him a saving sacrifice for us. You raised him from the dead and seated him at your right hand. You sent the promised Holy Spirit to power the church across the ages.

All this tells me, faithful God, that I may trust you. You will not forsake your people. You will not abandon us. You have saved us before. You will do it again. Your love is steadfast to the end. You are our refuge, our fortress, our everlasting rock.

I am not oblivious, O God. I see life's troubles. I know about hunger and thirst, sickness and death. I know cruelty and the terrible suffering it causes. I often have no idea why you permit as much trouble as you do. But I am trusting that this is due to my ignorance and not to any flaw in your character. I am dismayed, but I am not destroyed. I am distressed, but I still trust you and your Son, Jesus. How could I not? Who else is there, finally?

Resourceful God, your people appeal to you for common grace in society to uphold its basic structures. We trust you, but we need to trust others, too. We must trust our spouse to be faithful, our friends to be loyal, our parents and children to be honorable. We must trust airline pilots to be sober, teachers to be intelligent, police officers to be just. We must trust banks to be honest, dentists to be skilled, food workers to be clean. Do your work in society, O God, so that our trust may be justified.

I will trust you this day, good God. In Jesus's name, *Amen.*

Evening

Dwell in me, O blessed Spirit.* Dismiss my other spirits, and dwell in me. Clean the house of my soul, and dwell in me. Fill me, move me, inspire me. Breathe new life into me. Blow away the ash of sorrow and desolation. Blow away the webs of sin and shame. Blow away the wisps of doubt and indecision.

Breathe on me, breath of God.

> I am empty; fill me.
> I am chilly; warm me.
> I am suffocating under the mound
>   of my unconfessed sin; revive me.

Fill me with life anew. Else my thoughts go stale. My prayers fall flat. My hopes go slack.

Faithful God, always you are calling. You call us back from dangerous schemes. You call us out from hopeless labyrinths. You call us forth to speak good news. Always you are calling because it is never too late for us to listen.

* This prayer echoes "Dwell in Me, O Blessed Spirit," #745; "Breathe on Me, Breath of God," #747; and "Spirit of the Living God," #749, in *Lift Up Your Hearts: Psalms, Hymns, and Spiritual Songs* (Grand Rapids: Faith Alive, 2013).

If we listen, what will we hear? If we go to our doctor, the words we hear will be diagnosis and prescription. If we go to our lawyer, the words will be counsel and advice. If we go to our mechanic, the words will be parts and labor. All these are good words, but they are not the words of eternal life. And so we go to you whose words are our food and drink forever.

God of Good Friday, your Son was obedient right through death on a cross, and his obedience may be ours if we will trust you. God of Easter, who brought back from the dead our Lord Jesus Christ, you will bring us with him if we hope in you. God of Pentecost, who burned the hearts of a corrupt generation with the fire of the Holy Spirit, you will burn in our hearts too if we love you. Faithful God, parent of prodigal sons and daughters, your magnetic love will draw us home for Jesus's sake. *Amen.*

Morning

Redeeming God, it's a new day and my thoughts turn to you. You are the one who saves. Always you are the one to strengthen a slack heart or to soften a hard one. You are the one to subdue a rebel or retrieve a runaway. You are good at saving. It's a big part of your glory.

Today I want to be observant. I know it's easier to float, or to drift, or to drowse. Not for me today. I want to pay attention. I want my radar on. Whether in person or online or in books or on TV, I want to see what's going on.

Watchful God, what might I notice today?

I might see a macho teen's chin quiver as he speaks of his sick young sister. I might notice

> the tone of reverence in a widow's prayer
> the feel of a velvet sleeve
> the scent of my dog's wet coat
> the taste of grilled portobellos

Good God, these are things I may appreciate. But some of what I see today will have real weight. It will have moral significance. I might witness a Christian friend absorb major irritants without letting them paralyze her. A politician telling a difficult truth. A world health official doing his duty in an emergency. A child going to the side of another child who has just thrown up. I want to bless these things today because I know that you will bless them.

Loving God, I might also see darker things today. A person responding bitterly to an innocent question. An institutional leader refusing to accept responsibility for his decisions. An online discussion that grows toxic after just three exchanges. A bully first causing his victim's anger and then blaming him for it. I want to lament these things today because I know you will lament them.

Holy God, today let me be observant enough to hate what is evil and to love what is good for Jesus's sake. *Amen.*

Evening

O God, so much of my life is shrouded. My understanding is dark. My motives are shadowed. The way into my future is dim. But you are my light, my help and salvation.

Before I sleep, I want to examine myself. Today,

> Did I react with compassion
>   or indifference to the misery I saw?
> Did I rejoice with the fortunate or resent them?
> Was I gratefully aware of your presence
>   or oblivious to it?
> Was I stingy or generous?

Gracious God, I'm sorry for what I did wrong today. Please forgive me. I'm glad for what I did right today. Please reinforce it and build it into my character for good.

Thank you tonight for so much in life that is wonderful. Thank you for refreshing rain and for all the growing food it waters. Thank you for fields of amber grain; rows of tender, lime celery plants; hillsides of grape vines; orchards of pear trees. Thank you for green grass, sandy beaches, shady forests, surging tides. Thank you for rolling hills and sunny valleys.

Thank you for old friends, dependable friends. For friends I may trust with my secrets, for those who keep on loving me even when I am irritating, for those I may lean on for wise advice.

Thank you for the church and her faithful ministries, for intelligent pastors and musicians, lovers of evangelism and social justice, lovers of Scripture. Thank you for mayors and governors, adoption and social relief agencies, public libraries and museums. Thank you for those who provide public transportation and communication services. You shine in all that's fair and honorable.

At the end of this day, I commend to you all who especially need your tender care. People who have been betrayed by a spouse or orphaned in an accident. Those who have failed at their job once again and face the loss of it. Those who didn't fail but are still being fired, and so are indignant. Those unemployed because of sickness. All who lick their wounds or grieve their losses.

O God, bless them and keep them and cause your face to shine on them this night, for Jesus's sake. *Amen.*

Morning

L ord Jesus Christ, I acknowledge you this morning as "God with us." You are God *with* us, so I may know you. But you are also *God* with us, so you are way beyond me. I may know you, but not comprehend you. I may know you, but not through and through. You are both majestic and down-to-earth.

Your down-to-earth humanity comforts me. It makes you approachable.

> You got tired.
> You needed to get away from it all
> and find solitude.
> You wept over your friend Lazarus's death.
> You needed to pray a lot.

You were fully God, but you did not flash your divinity around town. You were measured. You cast out some demons, but not all. As far as we know, you turned water into wine just once. You invited just one disciple to walk on water. You raised Lazarus, but other bodies stayed in the ground that day.

You were steadfast. You were a friend to Peter, who was not always a friend to you. You were impressed by babies, telling your disciples that they ought to be like them. Babies can't do anything, but you knew they were perfectly wonderful receivers. Babies receive love and nourishment and simply live off them. And you said you want us to be like that when it comes to receiving the kingdom of heaven.

Your high priestly prayer amazes me.* You are only hours away from the time Judas and the soldiers will meet you with their torches and weapons, and what do you do? You pray for your disciples. Protect them, you pray. Sanctify them. Unite them. Fill them with joy.

Your prayer is thrilling in its power and beauty. You pour yourself out for your disciples while your own life is hanging by a thread. And in this I behold your glory. You do whatever it takes, pay whatever it costs, give whatever you've got so that we may have abundant life. Such remarkable goodness. Thank you. *Amen.*

* John 17.

Evening

Righteous God, you love fair wages, honest ads, right treatment. So, anoint prophets to do justice and love kindness. Sacrificial God, you gave up peace to create us, and you gave up your Son to save us. Anoint priests to offer up a sacrifice of praise. Sovereign God, supreme ruler, you share your regency with human creatures. Anoint kings to serve under your reign, making your purposes their own. O God, if I may be bold to ask, anoint me to be a prophet, priest, king.

Loving God, inspire us all to see deeply into the needs of the world and then to address them. If we are busy, inspire us to be busy with the needs of the world. If we are weary, let our weariness come from struggling with the needs of the world. If we are discouraged, inspire us to see that the world is yours and that you will one day fulfill the needs of the world and reconcile all things through Jesus Christ our Lord.

You have made our vocation clear. You call us to do justice, to love kindness, and to walk humbly with you.* We confess to you that our response to your call is spotty.

* Micah 6:8.

We have become indifferent to corruption.
We sometimes treat kindness as a weakness.
We walk arrogantly in the world, as if our lives
were our own.

Cleanse, forgive, and redirect us, O God.
God of our future, let us live as we will live when
your kingdom fully comes.

With our family members, let us live in love.
With our friends, in warmth.
With our fellow church members, in faith.

Meanwhile, move mightily among the nations, displacing tyranny and establishing peace. In our lives, with our families, in church, among the nations, be glorified.

Take us as we are, O God, but make us what we should be in the world you love. Make us salt and yeast and light. Make us prophets, priests, and kings. Make us agents, witnesses, and models of kingdom life, through Jesus Christ our Lord.

Now let me sleep in union with him. *Amen.*

Morning

Marvelous God, your grace for sinners is extravagant. You have a fullness of grace, an overflow of grace, an outpouring of grace—all for us sinners. The prodigal son was lavish in his spending, but you are lavish in your grace. I confess in amazement that I cannot out-sin your grace.

This day is full of promise, if only I will see it. Put me in a springtime mood, O God. When flowers adorn the earth, when the time of singing comes around again, when you dazzle me with colors and tantalize me with the fragrance of peonies, you remind me that you are a God of beauty. I want to see and hear and taste and touch and smell that the whole earth is full of your glory.

Surprising God, catch me off guard today. Arrest me with some glimpse of your splendor. Make your way past my boredom, my defiance, my indifference, my resentment. Make your way past all my nervous little defenses and speak to me. Speak, O God. Your servant is listening.

I pray with all your other children this morning. You are holy beyond all human knowing, and yet you are present to us, who are badly divided. We cling to you but also flee from you. We humbly receive your forgiveness but privately believe we do not need it so much. We do love you, but we love ourselves and our friends even more. Some of us are Christians by conviction, but some by convention. So, rebuke, correct, and heal us.

Have your way with us, O God.

> Our faith so often thins down. Enrich it.
> Our good intention so often wobbles. Steady it.
> Our determination to do what's right
>   so often sags. Shore it up, O God.

When we forget you, make yourself big and unmistakable to us again, through Jesus Christ our Lord. *Amen.*

Evening

God of the good creation: sun, moon, and stars bear witness to your power. The depths of the sea, the roll of the hills, the gentleness of a breeze bear witness to your fertile imagination. The faith of saints, the courage of martyrs, the voices of singing congregations bear witness to your stirring presence. The whole earth is full of your glory.

God of the wronged and wounded, some of us live too comfortably amidst grave oppression. We don't ask about it, look into it, fight against it. We are indifferent to it. O God, champion of the forgotten, forgive us, we pray, and kindle in us a new hunger for justice.

We confess to you that we are double-minded people.

> We love you, but we love money too.
> We love you, but we love worldly comforts too.
> We love you, but we love ourselves too.

In our folly, we more often think of ourselves than we think of you. In your mercy, center our minds on you, so that we are double-minded no more. You want truth within. Purify our hearts so that, knowing the truth, we may speak it, and, speaking the truth, we may follow up with actions that fit.

Surprising God, you come at us from directions in which we are not looking. You come at us when we are least expecting you. Stagger us with your goodness so that each day we find wonder upon wonder and every wonder true.

Strengthen our loves, O God. Shore them up, stake them down, push them out to you and to neighbors. We want to love you with everything we have. We want to love our neighbor as ourselves. We want to be better lovers today than we were yesterday.

Physician for the wounded and comforter of the desolate, your people across the world plead today for your healing touch.

> Some are discouraged; hearten them.
> Some are persecuted; liberate them.
> Some are impoverished; prosper them.

Merciful God, so many need your healing touch tonight. Make the wounded whole, through Jesus Christ our Lord. *Amen.*

Morning

Generous God, you told Israelites not to strip their vineyard bare or pick up its grapes from the ground, but to leave fruit for the poor. You gave poor people a stake in the Israelites' prosperity. And Jesus taught us what he heard from you, that to inherit the kingdom we must practice hospitality. Feed the hungry, satisfy the thirsty, welcome the stranger, clothe the naked, care for the sick, visit the prisoner.

Your Son himself left us an example. He multiplied loaves and fish for hungry crowds. On the night he was betrayed, he broke bread and poured wine for his disciples, even Judas. After his resurrection he invited his disciples to have breakfast with him on the beach. And he told stories of a father who had prepared a feast to welcome home his prodigal son, and of a good Samaritan who bound up the wounds of a stranger.

Jesus learned his hospitality from you, and I want to follow suit. Let me today pass a dish of food to someone and think of the act as sacramental. Let me bless people by passing to them what will help them thrive. Let me make room for others in my life and help them thrive in the room that I've made. Even if I should be confined to home or bed, O God, I can still pray to you for the good of so many.

Above all, I want to open the door of my heart when you knock on it.

Thank you for the heroes of hospitality who have left an inspiring mark on human life. The deacons who established the great hospitals of Europe and the hospices for pilgrims. The businesspeople who built safe facilities for homeless children and made them so warm and beautiful that the children were sad to leave. The gentiles who hid Jews from the Nazis and did it at great peril to their own lives.

Generous God, you make room for sinners and remake them in your image. You are a center of hospitality, and I want to imitate you for Jesus's sake. *Amen.*

Evening

Almighty God, great deliverer, you turn to us when we call.

> From snares and traps
>   you preserve us.
> From the downward spirals of sin
>   you save us.
> From life about to come unhinged
>   you deliver us.

We offer you our sacrifice of praise and prayer.

Author of each distinct human life, you imagined the children of the world from all eternity. Each of them is your unique thought. Each is unrepeatable, irreplaceable, irresistible. O God, each is a child of blessing, a child of your love, a child of joy.

Maker and keeper of promises, provide loving parents for children in homes made glad by your blessing. Surround them with singing, prayer, and the blessed Word. Give them good friends to grow up with. Provide the Holy Spirit to nudge them along right paths. Eternal God, maker and keeper of promises, secure these children in your fold forever.

We confess to you tonight that we are too often

foolish people. In both body and soul, we consume what isn't good for us. Break our bad habits and fill us with hunger and thirst for what truly satisfies. Fill us with hunger and thirst for your living Word and for the body and blood of Jesus Christ your Son.

Faithful God, you hold out blessing to us if we will take it with willing hands. But our hands reach elsewhere. You show us riches in great abundance if only we will see them. But our eyes look elsewhere. You speak solace to us if we will listen. But our ears listen elsewhere. You make and keep your promises, but our thoughts are too often elsewhere. So, tonight, we confess our sin and seek your gracious forgiveness.

Gracious God, whatever is true within us, whatever is noble, whatever is right, whatever is pure, whatever is lovely, whatever is admirable; if anything is excellent or praiseworthy in us,* we offer it all to you.

As I fall asleep, I'll be giving thanks for your tender care in Jesus's name. *Amen.*

* Paraphrase of Philippians 4:8–9.

Morning

Steadfast God, your abiding presence is the one still point in a tumultuous world. Cliffs may crumble, but you are with us. Nations may rage, but you are with us. Tyrants may rise and fall, but you are with us.

May your kingdom come a little closer today. Bring your loving rule a little nearer, O God. Let peace break out today. Inspire great, patient leaders to wage peace.

> Cool the world's hot spots.
> Calm and scatter its aggressors.
> Discourage efforts to wedge people apart.

I confess to you, O God, that we Christians don't always long for the coming of your kingdom. We whisper our prayers for the coming of your kingdom so that you can barely hear them. "Your kingdom come," we say, and hope it won't. When our own kingdoms have had a good year, we don't necessarily long for your kingdom to break in.* We like our own setup just fine.

Today let me imagine myself with people who are having a bad year. And have little hope of a better one. Let me stand with women who lack the cultural clout

---

*Justo L. González, *Alabadle!* (Nashville: Abingdon, 1996), 18.

106

to say no to promiscuous, infected men. In my heart, let me today stand with people crushed by poverty or injustice. Through them, let me start hungering for your kingdom to come.

Let me look around today so I can spot and celebrate the signs of your kingdom coming closer. What might I see today, good Lord? A hospital staff striving mightily for healing? A nation reforming its government? A film in which religious people are actually respected? A mom showing almost unearthly patience with her two-year-old?

Let me add my bit today. Let me hunger for justice and then do it. Let me show compassion. Let me write an encouraging note or say an uplifting word. Once again, let me live today in such a way that on your great day of judgment I can look back on *this* day and not be ashamed. In Jesus's name, *Amen.*

Evening

God of mercy, I'm praying with your people tonight. Hear our prayer. Bring peace to earth again. You sent your Son to bring forward your peaceable kingdom. Bring peace to earth again. You sent your heavenly hosts to proclaim peace on earth to those on whom your favor rests. Bring peace to earth again. You sent your Spirit to pour out the fruit of love, joy, and peace. Bring peace to earth again.

With you, good God, I journey in difficult times. I confess that I have no resources of my own to get me through. I am not tough enough, not pure enough, never wise enough to make my own way. But I am with you, so that I am no longer a wanderer but now a pilgrim on the way to my true home.

Thank you for your faithful love. You have steady enthusiasm for your children. You look on us with eyes of compassion. You incline your ear to hear us. You reach for us with hands of mercy.

Wonderful God, your favor comes to us in so many ways. Tonight, we give you thanks that your ten commandments are a form of the gospel. They give us the right recipe for a good life. They invite us to thrive. When we refuse to follow your commandments, it's *freedom* we're refusing. It's *grace* we're refusing. So, thank you that you have shown us how to live a good life and how to live it in abundance.

O God, we chafe under your commandments when we ought to be reveling in them. Make us teachable people, glad to learn your blessed recipe for abundant life. Make us humble enough to think we have something to learn from your Word. Then let us delight in your good teaching. We pray to you for basic wisdom, the knack of living effectively within your world.

Soon it will be time to sleep. Push away dreams of danger and disorder and bring forward dreams of beauty and longing. In Jesus's name, *Amen.*

Morning

Thank you, good God, for awakening me to this new day. Thank you for the promise it holds. Across the world, may this day be profitable for your purposes.

Let me grow in spiritual wholeness and maturity today. Strengthen my relationships with you, with others, with all creation. Stir my longing for you and your beauty, for Christ and Christlikeness, for other human beings. Let me love them and be loved by them. Stir my longing for your good creation, for its beauties and graces, for its sheer particularity. When my longings dim, let me long to long again.

Grow my love of your Word. Root it in my heart. Let me absorb it deeply and live off it. Encourage and comfort me with your Word. But also warn and direct me by it.

Dependable God, make me dependable. Let me keep my promises, sticking with people I'm stuck with and coming through for them when I'm needed.

Strengthen my faith. Give me the confidence that if I let myself go for you, I will get myself back. Give me faith in your mercies, that they are strong and tender and enduring. Let my faith in your goodness trigger gratitude that prompts me to serve others gladly. Let me take an interest in boring persons, ponder the lives of the great saints, spend time and money on just causes. In society, let me be willing to be overlooked.

Discipline my life today by Scripture and prayer, by solitude and meditation, by steady awareness of your loving presence. By these disciplines, free me from the rush of needs and urges and distractions. Make discipline the very basis of my freedom. Then, let my free and disciplined life become a kind of music I may offer to others.

Today, I give up claim to my towering ambitions. I give up claim to my foolish dreams. I give up claim to hopes and plans that do nothing for your kingdom. In Jesus's name, *Amen.*

Evening

To you, great God, I lift my heart to celebrate your love. You brought your people out of Egypt with a mighty arm. You pulled your people through wilderness and exile. You sent your Son to die and to rise from the grave in a second exodus. With praise and thanks, I turn to you, O God, and lift my heart to celebrate your love.

Wise God, discerner of the devices and desires of human hearts, you know the way your people need to walk. You know whose counsel we need to heed. In your mercy you have entrusted us with your holy Word to guide us in good paths by sound counsel. For this solid provision we give you hearty thanks.

We know your words, precepts, commandments, and laws. We know them and then we do what we want. What we so often don't understand is that we need your law in our sinew, and bone, and marrow. We need to be people who not only don't disobey you but who *wouldn't* disobey you, wouldn't even dream of disobeying you. So, plant your law in our hearts, O God. Plant it down deep so that its growth becomes the measure of our own.

Spirit of God, you ignite holy desire within human hearts. Make our hearts your hearth. Light up our desire for a taste of heaven. Kindle our desire for each other, which otherwise grows cold. Spirit of God, lighter of flames at Pentecost, ignite the fire of love in us all.

Eternal God, who spans the ages, we want to be faithful in our own age. We want to tell strangers the good news of the gospel, but first we want to tell our daughters. We want to tell friends the good news of the gospel, but first we want to tell our sons. If we are without children, we want to tell everyone the good news of the gospel. But first we want to tell those we love. In Jesus's name, *Amen.*

Morning

Noble God, among your people you are famous for your goodness. You have created a variety of fruits. Given apples, we probably didn't need peaches and pears. But you have created them too, just to delight us with choices. Thank you for all the varieties you have made—of trees and flowers and vegetables and animals and planets and bodies of water.

You make refreshing rain to fall on the fields of good people, but also on the fields of bad people. You pay special attention to widows, orphans, refugees, and the poor. You regenerate us by your Spirit and feed us with your Word. You forgive us sinners and clothe us with the righteousness of Jesus. Your goodness is beyond anything we could ask for, imagine, or deserve.

At the cusp of this new day, I am reveling in the thought of your human creatures across the world who will today do good works. They may be Christians, or they may not, but by your grace they will do good. In Asia, Africa, Europe, North America, South America, Australia, and Antarctica, people will today get after their programs of good deeds. They will reflect your own goodness as they help the world to flourish a little more.

I commend to you all the good they will do. Spouses encouraging each other, cooking for each other, running each other's errands. Parents embracing and nourishing their children. Friends supporting and gifting each other. Citizens paying taxes and voting. Church members providing soup for the sick, rebuking sexist remarks, telling the truth even when it's difficult to do it. People across the world taking good care of animals and of trees and shrubs. People shoveling snow or raking leaves or cutting grass for the elderly, the grieving, those with disabilities. People deliberately guarding each other's reputations. People rebuking racist remarks or bigoted comments on sexual minorities. Working on forgiving people who have hurt them. Planting trees that will shade future generations.

Good God, in Asia, Africa, Europe, North America, South America, Australia, and Antarctica, inspire billions to do good works today that make you believable. In Jesus's name, *Amen.*

Evening

Loving God, you sent your Son into the world that the world might be saved through him. You are the God of abounding grace, of ceaseless grace, of grace upon grace. Grace is your specialty. Grace is what you are known for. Your people need it now, holy God, because we are not pure within, and our sin rises to accuse us. We sin and then we accuse ourselves, abuse ourselves, indict ourselves because we simply are not pure within. So, save us from our sin, from ourselves, from sin that makes misery and misery that makes sin—save us from the whole wretched mess. On your grace we rest our plea.*

Creator of galaxies, you boom and crackle in summer storms. Your power is great, but so is your goodness that fills the earth with food. Your power and your goodness are great, but never greater than your love for sinners through Jesus Christ.

Lover of life, you give us sweet air and clean water. You give us healthy gardens to walk in. You are the God of seedling and plant, of snow and ice, of sun that melts

---

* See "God, Be Merciful to Me," #623, in *Lift Up Your Hearts: Psalms, Hymns, and Spiritual Songs* (Grand Rapids: Faith Alive, 2013).

snow. You are the God of birds chasing birds and of puppies chasing their tails. Let us respect your good creation and touch the earth lightly as we tread.

I commend to you all who faithfully did their jobs today. Thank you:

> for those who changed oil, sold tires,
> installed brakes
> for men and women who took temperatures
> and checked blood pressure
> for accountants, bankers, stockbrokers,
> insurance agents, who dealt honorably
> with people's money and security
> for painters, sculptors, and curators,
> who created or displayed beauty
> for prisoners in prison shops, for guards who
> treated them fairly, for wardens who ordered
> flowers to be planted in prison yards
> for occupational therapists who helped patients
> function better in daily life
> for men and women who honorably legislated,
> governed, and judged today

They did their job and now deserve their rest.
Thank you for all of them. In Jesus's name, *Amen.*

Morning

Merciful God, your forgiveness of sinners is a signature mark of your grace. Your Word tells us that you do not remember our sins, that you remove them, blot them out, tread them underfoot, cast them into the depths of the sea. Our sins are odious to you, so you want them gone.

Then you reconstrue us. We're no longer simply sinners. You now see us in Christ, united with him, justified by his death and resurrection, cloaked with his obedience, covered under his policy. You grant to us the perfect righteousness of Christ, as if we had never sinned nor been a sinner, as if we had been perfectly obedient.*

Your forgiveness and reconstrual of us can only be called amazing grace.

Let me today carry a forgiving spirit into the world. Let me soften my hard heart, soften my resentments, soften my outlook on those who have offended me. Let my gratitude to you for being forgiven drive my forgiveness of others. Let my forgiving attitude be a ligament of unity within the Christian community of forgiveness. Let it help to make the church a model of generosity within a skeptical world.

* *Heidelberg Catechism*, Q&A 60.

I know that my ability to forgive will be your gift. But I know it's also my calling, and not an easy one. Putting to death my old self, with all its hard-hearted resentments and grudges, is tough, but your Word tells me it opens the door for my new self to come forward. I want to travel the world today in my new self, with its love, joy, and peace. Let me, like you, reconstrue those who have offended me, seeing them as your image-bearers, seeing that they are, after all, human beings you love. Were they entirely to blame, O God? Was I partly complicitous? As a Christian charged with loving my enemies, shouldn't I at least wish them well?

O God, supreme forgiver of sinners, let me today imitate you with all sincerity and faith, through Jesus Christ. *Amen.*

Evening

Your people give you thanks tonight, imaginative God, for the treasures of your good creation. For each flower that opens, each little bird that sings, every joyous river that runs—for "all things bright and beautiful, all creatures great and small"*—we thank you with glad hearts. God of land and sea, of oil and wine, of peace and plenty, God of victory over sin and death, we thank you for who you are and acclaim your holy name.

Great God, sometimes you speak but sometimes you fall silent. Sometimes you prevent evil but sometimes you permit it, and we struggle to understand why. You chose Israel to bless the nations of the earth and had to live with her in wilderness and exile. In Jesus Christ you entered our world to save it. Your ways are deep, O God, but sweet in the end.

Living Breath of God, you who brooded over the waters at creation, come now, and fill our spirits. Living Breath of God, you who conceived Jesus by the Virgin Mary, pour out your gifts in abundance. Living

---

* From the hymn "All Things Bright and Beautiful," #20, in *Lift Up Your Hearts: Psalms, Hymns, and Spiritual Songs* (Grand Rapids: Faith Alive, 2013).

Breath of God, you who groan for the redemption of the whole creation, breathe in us tonight.

Lord Jesus Christ, your glory shines from the whole creation. You are the light of the world and the light of our souls. You bring joy to the world and joy to our hearts. Yours is the glory and honor, now and forever.

Father of Jesus, as I know from my own case, you daily suffer fools who ignore you. You set good laws and limits for us, but we transgress or ignore them. But you do not abandon us, even in our folly. Give us wisdom to honor your boundaries. Your prohibitions come from love. Your law comes from mercy. Give us wisdom to honor your lines, your limits, your sturdy laws, so that, inside them, we may thrive forever.

Tonight, I commend to your care all those I love, especially _____ and _____ and _____, all people in Christ, the whole troubled human race. We need you. In Jesus's name, *Amen.*

Morning

L ord Jesus Christ, enemy of darkness, you did not hold yourself above human evil but entered it, suffered from it, died to atone for it. I trust and thank you. Because of your love, you absorbed great evil. The sign of your love is your blood shed for sinners. It will never lose its power.

Your courage inspires me. You showed strength in the face of trouble. You ministered despite the ignorance and scorn of your own people's religious leaders.

> You were good to Peter, who denied you.
> You fed the last supper to Judas,
>   who betrayed you.
> You went on loving the disciples,
>   who deserted you.
> You forgave the men who crucified you.
> You reassured Thomas, who doubted you.

You were a man of sorrows and acquainted with grief, but you were also a man of immense and stirring courage.

Bless people across the world today who struggle to find the strength to face their troubles:

those who care for people with dementia
people trapped in paralyzed bodies
children trying to be brave after a parent
    abandoned them
bullied middle schoolers
seventeen-year-olds resisting the temptation
    to complete suicide
civil rights workers who persist nonviolently
    in the face of taunts, blows, and curses

Lord Jesus Christ, lend your courage to them all. Somehow let them know they are not alone. Give them an uncanny peace in the face of trouble. Be their strength and salvation.

Be mine too. I am not naturally brave, but if you are beside me today, I will manage. Give me courage to go straight forward. Clear a path. I don't know the way ahead, but you do. You know where I must go, and when, and how fast. Lord Jesus Christ, I want to step forward, but always behind you. In your strong name, *Amen.*

Evening

God of justice, you defend the cause of the voiceless. God of compassion, you weep with those who weep. God of the greatest humility, you emptied yourself in Jesus Christ to take the form of a servant. Your people want to be your image in the world, so that in seeing us people are reminded of you.

We want no longer to welcome bad news about famous citizens, but to receive it with sorrow and humility. We want no longer to resent good news about famous citizens, but to receive it with joy and thanksgiving. We want no longer to be fascinated with the idols of this age, but to resist them with conviction and resolve. Holy God, hater of wrong and lover of right, you shun all evil ways. Your people want to be your image in the world.

Ruler of nations, in troubled times we need faith to believe. We see trouble everywhere—slavery, murder, terror, war. We see the weak overpowered and the helpless abused. We see abusers get away with their awful behavior. We see terrorists untouched by international justice. Give us faith, O God, that in the end goodness is stronger than evil and love stronger than hate.

Comfort those who today faced into their troubles:

refugees
parents of children with serious disabilities
soldiers fighting justly for liberation
police officers who don't know who's
    behind the door they are knocking on
firefighters
those who choose what's right
    despite misgivings
persecuted Christians
those with depression
people facing a death they do not want

Great God, your people are hungry to hear you. At creation you spoke whole worlds into being. You spoke to Moses as one speaks to a friend. You spoke warning and comfort through the prophets. You spoke at last through the Word made flesh. Speak to us again, great God. Speak. Your servants are listening. In Jesus's name, *Amen.*

A Sunday Prayer

Good God, today on seven continents innumerable
congregations will worship you. In thousands of
languages, they will offer prayers of praise, confession,
thanksgiving, lament, petition, intercession, and dedi-
cation. They will

> hear your word,
> receive portions
>   of the loaf and cup,
> give their gifts,
> sing your praise,
> witness baptism, and
> hear that their sins are forgiven
>   and that they are right with you.

Many will worship online. Worshipers will include
children, teens, young adults, middle-aged folks, and
the elderly. They will be new Christians, veteran Christians, and not a few almost Christians, trying out worship for the first time. Most will be mindful that you
are our incomparable superior—our great creator, redeemer, and guide for life.

O God, those of us who worship would feel pangs
if we abstained. Worship completes and fulfills us.
More important, worship is for us right and fitting

and proper. It reaffirms our place in your universe. It acknowledges our sheer dependence on you.

It is fitting for us to praise you: for your creative energy that has dug out the depths of oceans and built in the strength of the hills; for your generous rains that moisten and soften the earth and for sunshine after rain that causes a part of your beauty to come across the earth in blooms and vines, in trees and shrubs. Above all, it is entirely fitting for us to thank you for the great salvation you have worked for us in the life, death, and resurrection of your Son, Jesus Christ.

O God, we look forward to the new heaven and earth that will stretch gloriously forward for eternity.

> Your justice will at last prevail over darkness.
> Your harmony will at last dispel chaos.
> Your peace will at last quiet unrest.
> And your love will at last wipe away all tears.

Then all nations and tribes and peoples will gather before you to acclaim your goodness and your mighty salvation. Every knee shall bow and every tongue confess that Jesus Christ is Lord, to your glory.* To your everlasting glory, forever. In Jesus's name, *Amen.*

* Paraphrase of Philippians 2:10, 11.

Acknowledgments

My colleagues John Witvliet, Kathy Smith, and Kristen Verhulst suggested that I write *Morning and Evening Prayers*. We work in the Calvin Institute of Christian Worship, and so a book of prayers lies naturally inside our mission. Thank you to them.

After I had a draft, I asked friends, family members, and colleagues to comment on it. Did they ever! Thank you to Robert Arbogast; Laura de Jong; Scott Hoezee; Mary Hulst; Peter Jonker; Daniel Migliore; Adam, Kathleen, and Nathan Plantinga; Mark Roeda; Kathy Smith; James Vanden Bosch; and Brian White. Their suggested edits have greatly strengthened the book.

Thank you to the good people at Eerdmans Publishing Company, including James Ernest, David Bratt, Jennifer Hoffman, Lydia Hall, and Meg Schmidt, who encouraged and shepherded the project at every stage.

"Lord, teach us to pray" is one of the oldest requests within the Christian faith. Like other Christians, I have been taught to pray by pastors, friends, parents, and authors. Their teaching has been golden. This book would not have been possible without it.